DISCOVERING CAREERS FOR YOUR FUTURE

fashion

Ferguson
An imprint of ☑®Facts On File

Discovering Careers for Your Future: Fashion

Ferguson
An imprint of Facts On File, Inc.
132 West 31st Street
New York NY 10001

Discovering careers for your future. Fashion.
    p. cm.
Includes bibliographical references and index.
    ISBN 0-8160-5568-8 (hc : alk. paper)
    1. Fashion—Vocational guidance. I. J.G. Ferguson Publishing Company. II. Facts On File, Inc.
    TT507.D57 2004
    391—dc22   2004005339

Ferguson books are available at special discounts when purchased in bulk quantities for businesses, associations, institutions, or sales promotions. Please call our Special Sales Department in New York at (212) 967-8800 or (800) 322-8755.

You can find Ferguson on the World Wide Web at http://www.fergpubco.com

Text design by Mary Susan Ryan-Flynn

Printed in the United States of America

EB FOF 10 9 8 7 6 5 4 3 2 1

This book is printed on acid-free paper.

Contents

Introduction

You may not have decided yet what you want to be in the future. And you do not have to decide right away. However, you may already know that you like fashion. Knowing your likes and dislikes is a great way to begin thinking about a career. Do any of the statements below describe you? If so, you may want to begin thinking about what a career in fashion might mean for you.

___I like to sew.
___I have a good sense of which colors go together and which do not.
___I enjoy sketching.
___I like to use my hands to make or build things.
___I work hard to make my school reports attractive.
___I make posters for my church or school.
___I enjoy photography.
___I often visit malls.
___I make my own clothes and jewelry.
___I like to give fashion advice to my friends and family.
___I enjoy putting outfits together.
___I like decorating my own room.
___I spend a lot of time using art and illustration programs on my computer.
___I enjoy drawing.
___I like to look at fashion magazines.
___I am interested in colors, shapes, and textures.

Discovering Careers for Your Future: Fashion is a book about careers in fashion, from costume designers to fashion models to photo stylists. Careers in fashion can be found on runways, in factories, in retail shops, in newsrooms, and in art studios. Some fashion designers create work that is considered pure art, while others design fashions that are more functional and are meant to be worn. While the fashion capitals of the world might by Paris, Milan, New York, and London, people around the world are interested in looking good and wearing clothes that make them feel attractive. Fashion workers make this happen.

This book describes many possibilities for future careers in fashion. Read through it and see how the different careers are connected. For example, if you are interested in modeling, you should read about fashion models, but also read about fashion designers, fashion models' agents, fashion photographers, makeup artists, and photo stylists. If you are interested in sewing, you will want to read the chapters on apparel industry workers, costume designers, knit goods industry workers, and tailors and dressmakers.

What Do Fashion Workers Do?

The first section of each chapter begins with a heading such as "What Buyers Do" or "What Personal Shoppers Do." This section tells what it is like to work at this job. It describes typical responsibilities and assignments. You will find out about working conditions. Which fashion workers design clothing? Which ones work at computers in offices? This section answers all these questions.

How Do I Become a Fashion Worker?

The section called "Education and Training" tells you what schooling you need for employment in each job: a high school diploma, training at a junior college, a college degree, or perhaps more. It also talks about on-the-job training that you can expect to receive after you are hired, and whether or not you must complete an apprenticeship program.

How Much Do Fashion Workers Earn?

The "Earnings" section gives salary figures for the job described in the chapter. These figures give you a general idea of how much money people with this job can make. Keep in mind that many people really earn more or less than the amounts given here because actual salaries depend on many different factors, such as the size of the company, the location of the company, and the amount of education, training, and experience you have. Generally, but not always, bigger companies located in major cities pay more than smaller ones in smaller cities and towns, and people with more education, training, and experience earn more. Also remember that these figures are current salaries. They will probably be different by the time you are ready to enter the workforce.

What Is the Future of Fashion Careers?

The "Outlook" section discusses the employment outlook for the career: whether the total number of people employed in this career will increase or decrease in the coming years and whether jobs in this field will be easy or hard to find. These predictions are based on economic conditions, the size and makeup of the population, foreign competition, and new technology. The U.S. Department of Labor and this book use terms such as "faster than the average," "about as fast as the average," and "slower than the average" to describe job growth predicted by government data.

Keep in mind that these predictions are general statements. No one knows for sure what the future will be like. Also remember that the employment outlook is a general statement about an industry and does not necessarily apply to everyone. A determined and talented person may be able to find a job in an industry or career with the worst outlook. And a person without ambition and the proper training will find it difficult to find a job in even a booming industry or career field.

Where Can I Find More Information?

Each chapter concludes with a "For More Info" section. It lists resources that you can contact to find out more about the field and careers in the field. You will find the names, addresses, phone numbers, and Web addresses of fashion-oriented associations and organizations.

Extras

Every chapter has a few extras. There are photos that show fashion workers in action. There are sidebars and notes on ways to explore the field, fun facts, profiles of people in the field, or lists of websites and books that might be helpful. At the end of the book you will find a glossary, which gives brief definitions of words that relate to education, career training, or employment that you may be unfamiliar with. There is an index of all the job titles mentioned in the book, followed by "Browse and Learn More," which is a list of fashion books and websites.

It is not too soon to think about your future. We hope you discover several possible career choices in the fashion industry in this book. Have fun exploring!

Apparel Industry Workers

What Apparel Industry Workers Do

Apparel industry workers produce, maintain, and repair clothing and other products made from cloth, leather, or fur.

The first step in making a garment is to take a designer's sample and make a paper pattern out of it. *Markers* make these patterns, usually with the aid of a computer. The pattern indicates cutting lines, buttonhole and pocket placement, pleats, darts, and other details. Computers also grade each pattern piece so it can be used for several size garments. Now the pattern is ready for mass production.

Cutters spread out fabric on cutting tables and cut material by hand or using machines. A cutting mistake can ruin yards of material, so cutters must be extremely careful.

Cut pieces of cloth are prepared for sewing by *assemblers*. Assemblers gather the various pieces needed for each garment, including lining, interfacing, and trimmings. They match color, size, and fabric design and use chalk or thread to mark locations of pockets, buttonholes, buttons, and other features.

Learn More about It

Bergh, Rene. *Kids' Clothes Sew Easy*. London: New Holland Publishers, 2003.

Milligan, Lynda, and Nancy Smith. *Best of Sewing Machine Fun for Kids*. Concord, Calif.: C&T Publishing, 2004.

Pam Bono Designs. *Quilt it For Kids: Quilts for Children of All Ages*. Concord, Calif.: C&T Publishing, 2000.

Simple Sewing: Complete Instructions for 7 Great Projects. Palo Alto, Calif.: Klutz, Inc., 1999.

A seamstress operates a sewing machine in a factory. (Corbis)

Sewers, who make up 70 percent of all apparel workers, use machines to sew together the loose pieces of fabric. Since a variety of sewing operations and machines are required for each garment, workers are classified by the type of machine and specific product on which they work. Workers are categorized into those who produce clothing and those who produce nongarment items such as curtains, sheets, and towels.

After the sewing operations have been completed, workers remove loose threads, basting, stitching, and lint. The sewn product may be inspected at this time.

Pressers operate automatic pressing machines. Some pressing is done as a garment is assembled; sometimes it is done at the completion of all sewing. Delicate garments must be pressed by hand.

Apparel inspectors and *production control technicians* monitor all stages of the production process and keep materials flowing smoothly. They detect defects in uncut fabric and semi-finished garments. They may mend these defects themselves or send them back for repair. Inspected finished clothing is then sent to the shipping room. From there, the product is sent to stores.

Tailors make garments from start to finish and must be knowledgeable in all phases of clothing production. *Custom tailors* take measurements and assist the customer in selecting fabrics. Many tailors work in retail stores where they make alterations and adjustments to clothing.

Education and Training

Few employers of apparel workers require a high school diploma or previous experience. However, courses in home economics, sewing, and vocational training on machinery are helpful. Having knowledge of computers is useful, since they are being used in many areas of production.

Apparel workers also need knowledge of fabrics and their characteristics, as well as good eye-hand coordination and the ability to perform repetitive tasks. They also must be able to work well with others and accept direction.

Earnings

The apparel industry is highly competitive, and low profits and wages are common. According to the U.S. Department of Labor, sewing machine

EXPLORING

○ Check out occupational information centers and catalogs of schools that offer programs for apparel workers.

○ Visit a clothing factory to observe the machinery and activities that go into making a garment. Try to talk to some of the apparel workers to gain insight about their jobs.

○ Work on a fabric project yourself or join an organization, such as 4-H, that offers such projects.

Words to Learn

bonding pressing fibers into a thin sheet and treating them with adhesive, heat, or solvent to hold the fibers together and form a fabric

crocheting using one yarn or thread and a needle with a hook on the end to create a series of connecting loops

knitting using several yarns or threads and two or more needles to create a series of interconnecting loops

lacemaking looping, interlacing, braiding, knotting, or twisting one or more threads to form a fabric with decorative designs

netting knotting or twisting thread or yarn together at regular intervals to form a mesh fabric with geometrically shaped openings

FOR MORE INFO

For information on the latest fashion market trends and news in the industry, contact
American Apparel and Footwear Association
1601 North Kent Street, Suite 1200
Arlington, VA 22209
Tel: 800-520-2262
http://www.americanapparel.org

For industry information, employment data, and educational resources, contact
American Textile Manufacturers Institute
1130 Connecticut Avenue, NW, Suite 1200
Washington, DC 20036
Tel: 202-862-0500
http://www.atmi.org

For career information, visit the following website:
Career Threads
http://careerthreads.com

operators generally earned a median salary of $17,440 in 2002. Patternmakers earned a median salary of $26,360; pressers, $17,070 a year; and custom tailors, $22,220 a year. Many workers in the industry are paid according to the number of acceptable pieces they turn out; therefore, their total earnings also depend on their skill, accuracy, and speed.

Outlook

Employment of apparel workers is expected to decline in the next decade. Increased imports and a heavier use of labor-saving machinery will reduce the demand for these workers. Apparel industry workers who have cross-trained and are capable of performing several different functions have a better chance at remaining in the field during periods of decline.

Buyers

What Buyers Do

Buyers select and purchase the merchandise that is sold in local and chain stores. Buyers often specialize in one kind of merchandise, such as clothing, jewelry, or toys. The goal of all buyers is the same: to find and buy the best products at the best price for the store or chain that employs them.

In some stores, buyers are responsible for both buying goods and supervising the selling of goods. In other stores, they are involved only with buying.

All buyers must be experts in the products they buy. Buyers order goods months before the store will sell them, and they must be able to predict how many will be sold. To do this, they must know all about the product—what it is used for, how well it is made, what it looks like, and who will buy it. Buyers must also know the best sources for purchasing the product.

When they make purchases, buyers need to have a clear understanding of what type of merchandise the store-owners prefer. For example, some store owners want to sell a large number of

Top Holiday Toys

Part of the buyer's job is to be able to predict what toys will fly off the shelves during the holiday season. In 2003, these toys were the hot items for buyers and consumers alike:

Barbie Cook with Me Kitchen (KIDdesigns)

Barbie in Swan Lake DVD (Mattel)

Beyblade Remote Control Top with Launcher (Hasbro)

BTR Transformers (Hasbro)

Care Bears Bedtime Lullaby Bear (Play Along)

Hokey-Pokey Elmo (Fisher-Price)

Bratz' Formal Funk Runway Disco (MGA Entertainment)

LeapPad Plus Writing Learning System (LeapFrog)

Leapster Educational Game System (LeapFrog)

McDonald's McFlurry Maker (Spin Master)

My Little Pony Celebration Castle (Hasbro)

NeoPets Voice-Activated Plush (Thinkway Toys)

Powertouch Learning System (Fisher-Price)

Source: *Toy Wishes Buying Guide* (http://www.toywishes.com)

lower priced goods. Other storeowners prefer to sell a smaller number of higher priced goods. Buyers must clearly understand how much profit the owners are trying to make. This will help them determine how much risk they are allowed to take in the type and quantity of products bought. If large quantities of goods do not sell, the store loses money.

A successful buyer must also understand what the customers are looking for. Buyers must stay up to date about what kinds of goods are popular, how much their customers can afford, and at what time the customers prefer to buy them. Buyers need to know the sizes, colors, and other features that will most satisfy their customers' needs. Buyers often work with *assistant buyers,* who spend much of their time maintaining sales and inventory records.

Education and Training

Most buying positions require at least a high school diploma. In high school, you should take courses in mathematics and English. If you go on to college, take courses in business administration, communications, marketing, retailing, purchasing, and economics.

Although college is not always required to become a buyer, you will have a better chance of getting a job with a bachelor's degree.

Earnings

A buyer's earnings will depend on his or her employer's sales volume. Mass merchandisers, such as discount or chain department stores, pay among the highest salaries.

EXPLORING

- Get experience in the retail field. Apply for a part-time job at a department store, boutique, or other retail shop.
- Explore door-to-door sales opportunities. Girl and boy scouts often organize sales drives to raise money for local troops. Your school might also need volunteers to help sell gift-wrapping paper, wreaths, cookbooks, or other goods to raise money.

Buying Concepts of Kids and Young Adults

Pre-schoolers have a basic understanding about buying things but little to no concept of value. Many think a nickel is more valuable than a dime because of its larger size.

Elementary school kids have more of an understanding of money, but may be careless in their decisions about it.

Pre-teens may view material goods as a way of gaining approval from their peers. Their self-image may be tied to the brand of clothes or shoes that they wear.

Teens seek out their own independence often through the goods they purchase. Their money skills are often in conflict with their parents' ideas.

Young adults that have some or most of their living expenses paid for by their parents often spend their earnings on luxuries. This economic freedom often comes to an abrupt end when they are forced to pay for their own living expenses.

Source: Ohio State University Extension Fact Sheet "Kids and Cash" (HYG-5216-96)

The U.S. Department of Labor reports the median annual income for wholesale and retail buyers was $40,780 in 2002. The lowest paid 10 percent of these buyers made less than $23,270 yearly, and at the other end of the pay range, the highest paid 10 percent earned more than $76,070 annually.

Outlook

The employment of buyers is projected to decline. This is because many businesses are merging, which results in the blending of buying departments. When this happens, people with overlapping job duties are often laid off. In addition, as computers continue to speed up business processes, there will be fewer new jobs for buyers. Some job openings will result from the need to hire replacement workers for those who leave the field.

FOR MORE INFO

For career resources, contact
Institute for Supply Management
PO Box 22160
Tempe, AZ 85285
Tel: 800-888-6276
http://www.ism.ws

For information on purchasing careers in the government, contact
National Institute of Government Purchasing
151 Spring Street, Suite 300
Herndon, VA 20170
Tel: 703-736-8900
http://www.nigp.org

For materials on educational programs in the retail industry, contact
National Retail Federation
325 7th Street, NW, Suite 1100
Washington, DC 20004
Tel: 800-673-4692
http://www.nrf.com

Costume Designers

What Costume Designers Do

Costume designers create the costumes seen in the theater, on television, and in the movies. They also design costumes for figure skaters, ballroom dancers, and other performers. During the planning of a show, costume designers read the script. They meet with directors to decide what types of costumes each character should wear for each scene.

Stories that take place in the past, called period pieces, require costume designers to have a great deal of knowledge about what people wore during different historical time periods in different parts of the world. Designers conduct research at libraries, museums, and universities to study the garments, shoes, hats, belts, bags, and jewelry that people wore. They look at the colors and types of fabric and how garments were made. Even for stories that take place in modern times or in the future, costume designers might use ideas that come from looking at the details of historical fashions.

Once their research is finished, designers begin to make sketches of costume ideas. They try to design each outfit to

Starting at the Bottom

One of ancient people's first articles of clothing was protective covering for the feet. Animal hides were ideal for this purpose. In warm climates, the typical footwear was the sandal, a sole with straps used to tie around the foot. In colder climates, people wore shoes that covered the whole foot and sometimes extended into boots. In ancient Greece and Rome, the soles of soldiers' sandals were studded with hobnails, or large-headed nails, for longer wear. Armies continued to use hobnail boots into modern times.

look authentic, or true to the time period when the story occurs. Designers also pay attention to the social status of each character, the season and weather for each scene, and the costumes of other characters in each scene.

Costume designers meet with directors for design approval. They also meet with stage designers and art directors to be certain that the furniture and backdrops used in scenes do not clash with the costumes. They meet with lighting designers to make sure that the lighting will not change the appearance of a costume's colors.

Depending on the production's budget, costume designers rent, purchase, or create costumes from scratch. They shop for clothing and accessories, fabrics, and sewing supplies. They also supervise assistants who sew or alter the costumes.

EXPLORING

○ Join a school drama club or a community theater. Volunteer to work on costumes or props. School dance troupes or film classes also may offer opportunities to explore costume design.

○ Learn to sew. Once you are comfortable sewing clothes from commercial patterns you can begin to try making some of your original designs.

○ Read *Glue & Go Costumes for Kids: Super-Duper Designs with Everyday Materials* by Holly Cleeland (New York: Sterling, 2004).

○ Practice designing costumes on your own. Draw sketches in a sketchbook and copy designs you see on television, in films, or on the stage.

Education and Training

To become a costume designer, you need at least a high school education, but a college degree in costume design, fashion design, or fiber art is recommended. You should also have experience working in theater or film.

English and literature courses will help you read and understand scripts. History classes are helpful for researching historical costumes and time periods. Courses in sewing, art, designing, and draping are also necessary.

Earnings

Costume designers who work on Broadway productions in New York

Don't Forget the Accessories

Costumes include a lot more than clothing. Designers have to also consider accessories, such as these:

- belts and girdles, including sword belts, sashes, and suspenders
- neckwear, such as ruffs, collars, cravats, neckties, and tie clasps
- eyeglasses, including monocles, lorgnettes, and pince-nez
- fans
- jewelry, including earrings, pins, necklaces, beads, bracelets, rings, and watches
- gloves
- purses and pouches
- shawls
- umbrellas and parasols
- walking sticks and canes

must be members of the United Scenic Artists Union. According to the union's 2004 minimum rates, a costume designer for a Broadway show with 36 or more characters must earn a minimum of $14,586. For off-Broadway shows, operas, and dance productions, salary is usually by costume count. For feature films and television, costume designers earn daily rates for an eight-hour day or a weekly rate for an unlimited number of hours.

Most costume designers work for themselves and are paid per costume or show. Costume designers can charge between $90 and $500 per costume, but some costumes, such as those for figure skaters, can cost thousands of dollars.

Outlook

Employment of costume designers is expected to decline in the next decade. Designers face stiff competition. There are many

FOR MORE INFO

This union represents costume designers in film and television. Visit the website for basic information on costume design.

Costume Designers Guild
4730 Woodman Avenue, Suite #430
Sherman Oaks, CA 91423
Tel: 818-905-1557
http://www.costumedesignersguild.com

This organization provides information on schools and college student memberships. Becoming a student member offers opportunities to network with other costuming professionals.

Costume Society of America
PO Box 73
Earleville, MD 21919
Tel: 800-272-9447
http://www.costumesocietyamerica.com

This union sets minimum wages for some costume designers.

United Scenic Artists
29 West 38th Street
New York, NY 10018
Tel: 212-581-0300
http://www.usa829.org

more qualified costume designers than there are jobs. Jobs will be hard to find in small and nonprofit theaters, due to smaller budgets and shows that require fewer costumes. There may be more costume design opportunities in cable television, which is growing rapidly and will continue to grow in the next decade. New York City and Hollywood are the hottest spots for costume designers.

Fashion Coordinators

What Fashion Coordinators Do

Fashion coordinators produce fashion shows and plan other ways to promote clothing companies and designers. They are employed by design firms, retail corporations, and apparel centers, and some work in the entertainment industry.

There are different types of fashion shows. Vendor or designer shows arrive at the fashion coordinator's office almost pre-packaged. The outfits are already accessorized and are boxed in the order the clothes should be shown. Commentary and backdrops also are supplied by the vendor or designer. To prepare for a vendor show, fashion coordinators only have to book models and set up a stage. Vendor shows typically take only a few days to produce.

Trend shows are put on by a retailer and are produced by the fashion coordinator and his or her staff. Coordinators put outfits and accessories together, choose the choreography and staging, and most importantly, decide on the theme or featured fashion trend. Trend shows are usually produced two or three times a year, and they take a few weeks or a month to produce.

There are several steps to producing a show. First, a budget for the show is set. Then models are selected. Coordinators often use modeling agents to find the best men, women, or children to show off the latest fashions.

Fashion Shows Online

Style.com, the online home of fashion magazines *Vogue* and *W*, has an entire section devoted to fashion shows. Visit this website to see photos from recent shows, critics' picks for the most popular looks, and more.

Style.com: Fashion Shows
http://www.style.com/fashionshows

Stylists are hired to give the models and their clothes a finished look. Hairdressers, makeup artists, and dressers prepare models before the show and during outfit changes. Production workers work to create the right music and lighting.

The fashion coordinator is also responsible for the promotion of a fashion show. They send invitations to the public and media and prepare advertising as well as set up chairs and props and check on other last minute details.

In addition to organizing shows, fashion coordinators promote their store's fashion lines through television, newspapers, and magazine exposure. Local television stations, newspapers, or fashion magazines sometimes borrow clothing from a store for a special shoot. The fashion coordinator pulls the appropriate clothing from the sales floor and delivers the chosen items to the TV station, newspaper, or magazine offices. The TV station or publication gives credit to the store in return for the use of the clothes.

Education and Training

High school classes that will prepare you for this career include family and consumer science, art, art history, illustration, photography, and business. Some schools, such as the Fashion High School in New York City, offer fashion-related courses such as fashion design, illustration, fashion merchandising, and art and art history along with the more traditional academic classes.

A college education is not required for every fashion job, but a bachelor's degree in fashion design and merchan-

EXPLORING

○ Watch fashion shows on television or read up on shows in fashion magazines. Take note of the style and themes used for shows and how they relate to the fashions presented.

○ Many high schools, colleges, and other community centers put on fashion shows. See if you can volunteer. You may be able to help models with outfit changes, set up chairs, or pass out brochures.

○ Produce a fashion show at your own school, using fellow classmates as models and clothing and accessories borrowed from family or friends.

Best of 2003

According to Fashion Wire Daily, these fashion designers (with the help of fashion coordinators) hosted the best shows of 2003:

○ Best Women's Fashion Show: Alexander McQueen. Based on Sydney Pollack's Depression-era drama, *They Shoot Horses, Don't They?*, McQueen's spring/summer 2004 show included dancers, singers, and models and required over two weeks of intensive rehearsals. The show featured patchwork designs and figure-hugging gowns with spangled bodices and huge feathered skirts.

○ Best Men's Fashion Show: Carol Christian Poell. Instead of strutting down runways, models floated down a Milan canal at sunset wearing items from the spring-summer 2004 collection.

dising, marketing, or other business-related courses will give you an edge. Computer skills are also important.

Earnings

There are no formal salary surveys available for this particular career. However, according to industry experts, most salaried stylists should expect to earn from $25,000 to $37,000 annually. Stylists working on a freelance basis can also earn as much, though they are paid only after a project is completed as opposed to weekly or bimonthly. Successful fashion coordinators employed by larger corporations or well-known design houses can earn over $100,000 a year.

Outlook

Employment in this career should be good for the next decade. Most jobs in the United States will be available in densely populated areas, especially New York City, Chicago, Los Angeles, and Miami.

As fashion trends change, so will runway shows. Show themes reflect the taste of the consumer. Flashy styles translate to loud, heavily choreographed shows. Conservative styles may call for softer presentations. One style of show has no spoken commentary. Instead, messages in words and images are shown on backdrops. More recently, the lingerie chain Victoria's Secret has produced shows for both TV broadcast and the Internet. These new and varied types of shows should provide employment opportunities for the creative fashion coordinator.

FOR MORE INFO

For information on the industry, student membership, or networking opportunities, contact

Fashion Group International, Inc.
8 West 40th Street, 7th Floor
New York, NY 10018
Tel: 212-302-5511
http://www.fgi.org

To learn more about the programs and exhibitions offered at FIT, check out the website or contact

Fashion Institute of Technology (FIT)
Seventh Avenue at 27th Street
New York, NY 10001
Tel: 212-217-7999
http://www.fitnyc.suny.edu

For art and design school rankings, visit the following website:

National Association of Schools of Art and Design
11250 Roger Bacon Drive, Suite 21
Reston, VA 20190
Tel: 703-437-0700
http://nasad.arts-accredit.org/index.jsp

Fashion Designers

What Fashion Designers Do

Fashion designers design coats, dresses, suits, and other clothing. A small number of designers work in the fashion centers of the world: Paris, New York, Milan, and London. These high-profile designers create styles that set fashion trends for each season. Most designers, however, work for textile, apparel, and pattern manufacturers. Some work for fashion salons, high-fashion department stores, and specialty shops. A few design costumes for the theater and movies.

Designers first figure out what their customers want and need. They make rough sketches and then draw flat pattern pieces on large sheets of paper. The patterns are laid on the fabric to provide cutting guidelines. Instead of using sketches, some designers prefer to work directly with fabrics on a dressmaker dummy. They use inexpensive fabric, such as muslin, and pin or stitch the material directly on the dummy. Fabric pieces are then removed and used to make paper patterns.

Once the final pieces are cut and sewn, designers fit them on a model. This sample garment is shown to buyers, and alterations are made as needed. In small shops, designers work on all phases of fashion production, from thinking up the original idea to sewing the completed garment.

Fashion Fundamentals

harmony   all parts of a fashion design should work together

proportion   all parts of an outfit should relate to one another in size, length, and bulk

emphasis   a garment should have one feature that attracts the eye

balance   a garment should have equal interest in all directions from the main center of interest

A team of fashion designers discusses a series of designs. (Corbis)

In larger companies, designers design and draw the original style, while the other work is left to patternmakers, graders (who draw the paper patterns in various sizes), and sewers.

Fashion designers who work for large firms that mass-produce clothing often create 50–150 designs for each season.

See Student Work

FIT (Fashion Institute of Technology) offers a website (http://www.fitnyc.suny.edu) that features pictures of fashion designs done by past and present students. From the home page, click on the link for Prospective Students and Visitors, then click on the Gallery link. Click the various Fashion Design links to browse galleries of live models and art sketches.

They work on spring and summer designs during the fall and winter months and on fall and winter clothing during the spring and summer months. Some designers work for a few individual clients. In fact, many designers start out this way. As their reputation and number of clients grows, so does their business, until they are creating a full set of designs for each new season.

Education and Training

The best way to become a fashion designer is to complete a two- or three-year program in design from a fashion school. Some colleges offer a four-year degree in fine arts with a major in fashion design.

Designers must be creative, have the ability to draw, and work well with their hands. Math skills are important for converting a flat pattern into a shaped garment, sizing patterns, and measuring yardage. Computer skills are also necessary because most designers use computer programs to create and alter their designs before even touching a piece of fabric.

EXPLORING

○ Practice your sewing skills. Start by using commercial patterns available at fabric stores. Frequent sewing will make you familiar with flat patterns and the various steps in clothing construction.

○ Art and design courses will help you work on your sketching and drawing ability, and develop your color sense.

○ Keep a sketchbook of fashion ideas. Collect fabric swatches and match them to the fashions you have drawn.

○ Visit fabric stores and look at the materials available, including fabrics, buttons, threads, ribbons, and other notions.

○ Attend fashion shows, visit art galleries, and observe clothing worn by fashion leaders.

Earnings

Fashion designers earn median annual salaries of $51,290. Salaries range from $25,350 to more than $105,280. A few highly skilled and well-known designers in top firms have annual incomes of more than $150,000. Top fashion designers

FOR MORE INFO

For listings of accredited design schools and information on choosing the best program, contact
National Association of Schools of Art and Design
11250 Roger Bacon Drive, Suite 21
Reston, VA 20190
Tel: 703-437-0700
http://nasad.arts-accredit.org/index.jsp

who have successful lines of clothing can earn bonuses that bring their annual incomes into the millions of dollars, but there are few designers in this category.

Outlook

According to the U.S. Department of Labor, employment of designers is expected to grow faster than the average for all occupations. Increasing populations and growing personal incomes should increase the demand for fashion designers. Good designers always will be needed, although not in great numbers. There are about 16,000 fashion designers in the United States, which represents less than 1 percent of the garment industry.

Fashion Illustrators

What Fashion Illustrators Do

Fashion illustrators use a variety of media (for example, pencil, pen and ink, or computer technology) to create illustrations that appear in print and electronic formats. Illustrations are used to advertise new fashions, promote models, and popularize certain designers.

Some illustrators provide artwork to accompany editorial pieces in magazines such as *Glamour, Redbook,* and *Seventeen* and newspapers such as *Women's Wear Daily.* Catalog companies also employ illustrators to provide the artwork that sells their merchandise through print or online publications.

Fashion illustrators work with fashion designers, editors, and models. They make sketches from designers' notes or they may sketch live models during runway shows or other fashion presentations. They use pencils, pen and ink, charcoal, paint, airbrush, or a combination of media to create their work.

In addition to working with pens and paper, fashion illustrators also need to be able to work with computer programs

Early Fashion Illustration?

Illustration featured prominently in the ancient civilizations of Mesopotamia, Egypt, and later Greek and Roman civilizations. Drawings of figures conveying power or ideas have also been found among ancient Assyrian, Babylonian, Egyptian, and Chinese societies. Modern illustration began during the Renaissance with the work of Leonardo da Vinci, Andreas Vesalius, and Michelangelo Buonarotti.

designed to manipulate their artwork. They should also have good business sense (especially if they work as freelancers) to be able to sell their work to employers, bill clients promptly and appropriately, and keep organized records of their work. Illustrators who work for magazines or newspapers may work long hours to meet print deadlines.

Education and Training

There are a number of classes you can take in high school to help you determine the extent of your artistic talent as well as prepare you for this work. Naturally, take as many studio art classes, such as drawing and painting, as you can. Computer classes that teach you about computer-aided design will also be useful. Business and mathematics classes will give you skills you will need to keep track of your accounts and run your own business. Take English or communication classes to develop your communication skills.

After high school, consider enrolling in a fashion illustration program at an art school, university, community college, or adult education center. An associate's or bachelor's degree is not necessary to become a fashion illustrator, but it will give you the opportunity to build a portfolio. A portfolio is a collection of an artist's best sketches to show to prospective clients.

EXPLORING

○ Join your school's yearbook, newspaper, or literary magazine. These publications often include student illustrations along with text.
○ Apply for a part-time job at an art supply or retail clothing store.
○ Read fashion magazines and websites that include fashion sketches to see what others are doing and to learn about the latest fashion trends and models.

Earnings

The U.S. Department of Labor reports that salaried fine artists, including illustrators, had median yearly incomes of approximately

Try It Yourself

The best way to see if you have what it takes to become a fashion illustrator is to start drawing. Use the following website to practice drawing basic modeling figures and read tips about using other materials such as glue, pens, and mounting boards:

Fashion Drawing Tutorial Tips
http://www.fashion-era.com/drawing_fashion.htm

$35,260 in 2002. Earnings ranged from a low of $16,900 to a high of $73,560. Their earning potential depends on where their work is published. A large fashion magazine is able to pay more for an illustration than a small publisher. Illustrators that build a strong portfolio of published work and work for more prestigious clients can make hundreds of thousands of dollars.

FOR MORE INFO

For information on college programs in fashion design, advertising, and design, contact
International Academy of Design and Technology-Chicago
1 North State Street, Suite 400
Chicago, IL 60602
http://www.iadtchicago.com

International Academy of Design and Technology-Orlando
5959 Lake Ellenor Drive
Orlando, FL 32809
http://www.iadt.edu

This national institution promotes and stimulates interest in the art of illustration by offering exhibits, lectures, educational programs, and social interchange.
Society of Illustrators
128 East 63rd Street
New York, NY 10021-7303
Tel: 212-838-2560
http://www.societyillustrators.org

Visit this site to view several examples of fashion sketches.
Metrofashion
http://www.metrofashion.com/sketches.html

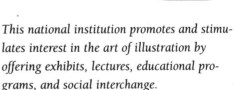

Outlook

Employment for visual artists is expected to grow as fast as the average during the next decade. The employment of illustrators specifically working in fashion will depend on the prosperity of magazines, newspapers, advertising firms, and fashion houses. The outlook for these employers currently looks strong. Competition for jobs, however, will be keen since these positions are highly attractive to people with artistic ability. Illustrators who are creative and persistent in finding job leads will be the most successful.

Fashion Models' Agents

What Fashion Models' Agents Do

Fashion models' agents are the link joining the talent (the model) with an employer (clients who have jobs for models). Agents match models to jobs according to the particular "look" the client desires.

An agent's job may begin when a client contacts the agency with a possible job assignment. The client, for example, a retail store, usually will have a specific look in mind for the model. The look may include such aspects as the model's hair color, age group, body type, or ethnicity. Once the look has been explained, the agent refers to his or her comp board, which displays pictures and information about the models represented by the agency.

The agent then sends a group of models that fit the desired look to the client for an audition. If the model is chosen for the job, then he or she is booked, or given the assignment.

In addition to finding models jobs, agents also arrange for the model's transportation if the assignment is out of town. They also type up call sheets. A call sheet is a notice containing all pertinent information about the modeling assignment, such as

Check These Out

Agents should be interested in fashion, since they need to stay current on the newest trends of the industry. To do this, agents frequently do a lot of reading during their free time, looking over such magazines as *Vogue* and *Seventeen,* or the trade newspaper *Women's Wear Daily.* Buy these publications at your local bookstore or view them online.

Seventeen
http://www.seventeen.com

Vogue
http://www.style.com/vogue

Women's Wear Daily (subscription required)
http://www.wwd.com

EXPLORING

○ Hone your selling abilities by getting a part-time or seasonal job at any retail store. Whether you are selling an article of clothing or a model's talent, what's important is your ability to market and sell a product.

○ Attend a model convention or search. Elite Modeling Agency, for example, conducts an annual "Look of the Year" contest held in several cities nationwide. You will be able to observe the process potential models go through as well as see agents at work.

whether it is a photo shoot, fashion show, or product demonstration. Location and time are listed on the call sheet, as well as how the model is expected to look, for example, full makeup and heavily styled hair versus clean face and hair.

While agents maintain good working relationships with established clients, they also look for new clients and more assignment possibilities. In addition, agents are continuously searching for new models. Modeling shows and conventions are held through the year all over the United States and abroad. Agents attend such shows to scout for models, interview them, and perhaps offer them modeling contracts.

Education and Training

A high school diploma is necessary for work as a fashion models' agent. While a college degree is helpful, you do not necessarily need one to get ahead in this industry. Much of the training is learned while on the job.

Take classes such as family and consumer science and art. Business and mathematics classes will help you later when working with modeling contracts and negotiating salaries. English and speech classes will help you develop your communication skills. If your high school offers any sales and marketing courses, be sure to take those. Some high schools offer curriculum targeted to fashion, which may include classes in design, illustration, and sewing. Sign up for these if they are available.

Ford Models: Fashion Industry Giant

In 1946, when Eileen Ford agreed to work as secretary for two model girlfriends, little did she know she was about to start an empire. For $65 a month, she provided her model friends with advice on clothing, makeup, and hair, as well as career planning and bookkeeping. Before long, models were flocking to be represented by Eileen Ford. Her husband Jerry soon joined in the business and became partner in what became the agency, Ford Models. Since its beginnings, Ford has represented thousands of models, some of whom achieved supermodel status, such as Christie Brinkley and Elle MacPherson. Currently, the agency is still headquartered in New York City, but it maintains offices worldwide. They represent female and male models in mainstream fashion as well as plus-sized, child, and teen models.

Earnings

Salaries for fashion models' agents vary depending on such factors as an agent's experience, the size and location of their agency, and the models they represent. New agents can expect to earn an annual starting salary of approximately $26,000. Those with previous agency experience can earn about $45,000 per year or more. Agents at the top of the industry may make $100,000 or more.

Some agents are paid on commission. This means they earn a percentage of the fees generated by model/client bookings. Commission rates normally range from 10 to 15 percent of model booking totals.

Outlook

Employment in this field should grow about as fast as the average in coming years. Since most clients prefer to work with

FOR MORE INFO

For information about this school, admissions requirements, and exhibitions of The Museum at FIT, contact

Fashion Institute of Technology (FIT)
Seventh Avenue at 27th Street
New York, NY 10001
Tel: 212-217-7999
http://www.fitnyc.suny.edu

For information about the modeling industry and a listing of modeling agencies in the United States and abroad, visit the following website:

The Insider's Guide to Supermodels and Modeling
http://www.supermodelguide.com

To read about fashions, models, and agencies, check out this website.

Models.com
http://models.com

modeling agencies, very few models succeed without the support of an agency. New York City will continue to be the hub of modeling in the United States. Many large agencies will stay headquartered there. Some model agents may find more jobs by representing actors and actresses. Other agents represent models who are hired for specific body parts. The most popular areas of specialization include legs, feet, or hands.

Fashion Models

What Fashion Models Do

Fashion models exhibit clothes and other accessories. They act in television commercials, pose for photographers and artists, appear in fashion shows, and help sell products in stores and at conventions. Many people know about the glamorous super-models who wear expensive clothing and have their pictures taken all over the world, but people of all ages and back-grounds work in this field.

Watch Out for Scams!

Though talent agents spot some models on the street, at the mall, or other public places, most models get their break by actively seeking out agencies. Therefore, be wary of anyone who approaches you about becoming a model. Follow these suggestions from the Federal Trade Commission (FTC) to prevent yourself from becoming the next victim of a modeling scam.

○ If you're approached by a so-called model agent, ask yourself, "why me?" Think about how many others also may have been approached.

○ Be wary of agencies that require an up-front fee to serve as your agent.

○ If an agency requires payments made in cash, be warned. The company is probably more interested in your money than your career.

○ Get all the agency's claims and promises about jobs, salaries, etc. in writing.

○ Do not sign a contract without reading and understanding it first. Take a copy of the con-tract home with you and review it with someone you trust. If the company refuses, walk away.

○ Ask for names and contact information of models who have worked with the agency. If the company refuses, walk away.

○ If the agency claims it has placed models and actors in specific jobs, contact the companies to verify that they've hired models and actors from the agency.

○ For more information, visit http://www.ftc.gov/bcp/conline/pubs/services/model.htm

Although the work may appear to be fun and exciting, it is demanding and difficult. Many fashion models pose for photographs or illustrations used in advertising brochures and sales catalogs. One photograph may be taken in a studio under hot lights with the model wearing a heavy fur coat. Another may be taken outdoors in cold weather with the model wearing only a bathing suit. One job may last an hour, while another may require an entire day. Fashion models may travel all over the United States and to foreign countries to be photographed in exotic or unusual settings.

In large stores, fashion models are employed to promote the sale of various products. The store may have a regularly scheduled fashion show during the lunch hour. These models walk down a runway modeling the newest clothing designs for consumers and store buyers. At other times, the models may walk throughout the store showing clothing or other apparel and talking with customers about the garments.

There are significant differences in the requirements necessary for each type of model. The major requirement for the fashion model is, of course, physical appearance. Although most people think of all models as being young and slender, that is not necessarily the case. No set standard exists for a model's physical description because many different body types are needed.

Specialty models must possess particular features that are photogenic, such as hands, feet, legs, hair, lips, or ears that will help sell specific products.

Models should be physically attractive but do not need to be extremely beautiful or handsome. They must

Models display the latest fashions at a runway show. (Corbis)

have a neat appearance and a pleasant personality and be able to work under stressful conditions. The ability to stay in good condition (getting the proper amount of sleep, keeping a strict diet, and exercising) also is important. Finally, the ability to handle rejection is critical because models often compete at auditions with many other qualified candidates for only one or two jobs.

Education and Training

There are no standard educational requirements for models. Most employers of photographic models prefer at least a high school education. Courses such as sewing, art, home economics, and photography are helpful.

There is no best way to become a model. Physical appearance and the ability to present clothing or products in an interesting manner are more important than educational background. Many

EXPLORING

○ Gather information from a variety of sources, including agencies, books, and articles.

○ Flip through some fashion magazines or watch the Style network. Watch how models carry themselves on the runway.

Learn More about It

Esch, Natasha. *Wilhelmina Guide to Modeling.* New York: Fireside/Simon & Schuster, 1996.

Marcus, Aaron R. *How to Become a Successful Commercial Model: The Complete Commercial Modeling Handbook.* Baltimore: Marcus Institute of Commercial Modeling, 1997.

Rubenstein, Donna, and Jennifer Kingston Bloom. *The Modeling Life: The One (And Only) Book That Gives You the Inside Story of What the Business Is Like and How You Can Make It.* New York: Perigee Books/Penguin Group, 1998.

Williams, Roshumba, and Anne Marie O'Connor. *The Complete Idiot's Guide to Being a Model.* New York: Alpha Books/Penguin Group, 1999.

FOR MORE INFO

For tips on getting into modeling, visit this website.
How to Model
http://www.howtomodel.com

For information on modeling careers and annual conventions, visit this website.
International Modeling and Talent Association
http://www.imta.com

To read about fashions, models, and agencies, check out this website.
Models.com
http://models.com

models attend modeling schools, where they learn the skills and techniques of the business. Others take courses in dancing or physical fitness to improve their health and learn to move more gracefully.

Earnings

Earnings for models vary according to their experience and depend on the number, length, and type of assignments they receive. Today, top fashion models working full time for wholesalers or retailers earn approximately $40,000 or more a year. Models working retail shows earn between $15,000 and $18,000 or more each year. Female models working for agencies make $100 to $125 an hour. Hourly wages are higher for photographic models working in large metropolitan cities such as New York, Los Angeles, or Chicago and for models who are in great demand. Top photographic models signed to exclusive contracts with cosmetic firms may earn $1 million or more per year. Almost all models work with agents and pay 10 to 15 percent of their earnings in return for an agent's services.

Outlook

Employment growth for models will be faster than the average through the next decade, but job competition will be fierce because this career is attractive to so many people. The number of fashion models seeking jobs is far greater than the number of openings. Part-time work is easier to find than full-time work. Most openings will occur as models quit or retire to pursue other employment or interests.

Fashion Photographers

What Fashion Photographers Do

Fashion photographers shoot pictures of the exciting world of fashion. They take and develop pictures of people, places, and objects while using a variety of cameras and photographic equipment. Photographs are used to promote fashions, models, and designers.

Advertising is probably the largest employer of fashion photographers. These artists create the pictures that sell clothing, cosmetics, shoes, accessories, and beauty products. Large retailers that publish catalogs of their goods also hire fashion illustrators to shoot images of models, clothing, shoes, and other merchandise. Some photographers work on staff or as freelancers for fashion magazines or newspapers.

In addition to being skilled at photography, fashion photographers should also be able to use new technologies such as digital cameras and computer programs designed to store and alter images. Photographers may work as freelancers, handling all the business aspects that go along with being self-employed. Such responsibilities include keeping track of expenses, billing clients, and keeping their businesses going by lining up new jobs for when a current project ends.

Because the fashion world is extremely competitive and fast-paced, photographers tend to work

> ### Agree or Disagree?
>
> Visit this site to read women's studies expert Karen Lehrman's opinions on the current state of fashion photography.
>
> **The Decline of Fashion Photography: An Argument in Pictures**
> http://slate.msn.com/features/010510_fashion-slide-show/01.htm

A team of photographers preps a model before a photo shoot. (Corbis)

long hours under the pressure of deadlines and demanding personalities.

Education and Training

If you want to become a fashion photographer, you have many training options. You may decide to study fashion design and work on your photography skills on the side. Or you could focus your studies on photography but also take some classes in fashion. In addition, there are full academic programs in fashion photography at many colleges and universities. Many community and junior colleges offer associate degrees in photography or commercial art. While a college degree is not required, these programs will help you develop your skills, meet contacts in the fashion or

EXPLORING

○ Take photography classes both at school and through local organizations such as community centers.
○ Join a school photography club.
○ Join the staff of the school yearbook, newspaper, or literary magazine.

An Interview with Frances Pellegrini

Frances Pellegrini shot fashion photography from the late 1940s through the 1980s. Among other publications, her work appeared regularly in *Glamour* and *Harper's Bazaar*. Read her interview and see her work at http://www.biddingtons.com/content/creativepellegrini.html.

photography industries and, most importantly, build up your portfolio. A portfolio is a collection of your best fashion pictures that shows employers the scope of your talent. A portfolio is almost always required when looking for a job in fashion photography.

Earnings

According to the U.S. Department of Labor, the median annual pay for salaried photographers was approximately $24,040 in 2002. The lowest paid 10 percent made less than $14,640, while the highest paid 10 percent made more than $49,920 per year.

Fashion photographers running their own businesses and working on a freelance basis are typically paid by the job. The pay for these jobs may be based on such factors as the photographer's reputation, the prestige of the client (for example, a fashion magazine with an international readership will pay more for photos than a local newspaper doing a Sunday fashion spread), and the difficulty of the work. For some of this work, photographers may make $250 per job. They may also get credit lines and receive travel expenses. As they gain experience, photographers can make $2,000 per job or more. Freelance photographers who have national or international reputations can make $100,000 or more per year.

FOR MORE INFO

For information on college programs in fashion design, advertising, and design, contact

International Academy of Design and Technology-Chicago
1 North State Street, Suite 400
Chicago, IL 60602
http://www.iadtchicago.com

International Academy of Design and Technology-Orlando
5959 Lake Ellenor Drive
Orlando, FL 32809
http://www.iadt.edu

This college offers programs in various art and design fields.
Savannah College of Art and Design
PO Box 3146
Savannah, GA 31402
Tel: 800-869-7223
http://www.scad.edu

This website allows you to browse through galleries of hundreds of established fashion photographers.
FashionBook.com
http://www.fashionbook.com/photographers

Visit this site for more career advice.
Fashion Net: How to Become a Fashion Photographer
http://www.fashion.net/howto/photography

Outlook

Employment for photographers in general is expected to grow at an average rate. The American fashion industry, due to its popularity around the world, is running strong. Magazines, newspapers, advertising firms, and fashion houses will always need trained photographers to capture the latest styles. Employment opportunities will also be found in new media outlets such as e-zines and retail websites.

However, the growing popularity of digital cameras and computer programs can allow consumers and businesses to produce and access photographic images on their own. Despite this improved technology, the specialized skills of the trained photographer should still be in demand in the fashion world.

Fashion Public Relations Specialists

What Fashion Public Relations Specialists Do

When a fashion house, retail company, or other organization that sells fashion items wants to present a good image to the public, it turns to its public relations (PR) department or to a PR firm. *Fashion PR specialists* include executives, writers, artists, and researchers. These specialists work together to provide information to the public about a company, its accomplishments, and goals for the future. Their work helps to promote the company's reputation in hopes of selling more clothing, shoes, jewelry, or other merchandise.

Fashion PR specialists spend much of their time writing. They write reports, news releases, booklets, speeches, and copy for radio and television ads. PR specialists also edit employee publications, newsletters, and reports to shareholders. All of

Museum of Public Relations Debuts Online

In late 1997, Spector & Associates "opened" the Museum of Public Relations on the Web. This online museum is meant to provide a history and examples of successful public relations programs for industry, education, and government, using photographs and stories. Read about such public relations trendsetters as Edward L. Bernays, Moss Kendrix, Carl R. Byoir, Arthur W. Page, and Chester Burger. For more information, visit http://www.prmuseum.com.

this writing and editing has one goal: to offer the public positive information about a fashion designer, house, or company.

Contact with the media is another important part of fashion PR specialists' jobs. They promote their company through radio, television, newspapers, and magazines. They also use special events to get their messages across. Press parties, fashion runway shows, and open houses help to establish good feelings and a positive image between the company and the public—its potential customers.

Most large retailers and fashion houses have their own public relations departments and hire their own workers. Other companies hire outside firms whose workers provide PR services to one or more companies. In either case, these workers must be specialists in not only PR, but in fashion trends as well. To keep up with the latest styles, PR workers do research or conduct public opinion polls. When conducting polls, fashion PR specialists ask random people questions about their interests. For example, a PR specialist might ask people of different ages what brands of clothing they buy. This research would analyze which fashions are popular among different age groups. From this information, they can develop a PR plan for their company and put it into action.

Education and Training

Most PR specialists are college graduates, so it is important to take college preparatory courses, especially English, speech, humanities, and lan-

EXPLORING

○ Develop your interpersonal skills by seeking out opportunities to work with other people.

○ Join your school newspaper or yearbook staff to work on your writing and reporting skills.

○ A job in clothing retail will give you fashion experience and help you to understand some of the principles of product presentation.

○ Volunteering to help with a political campaign can expose you to how PR specialists use persuasive speaking and writing tactics and how they deal with the media.

Profile: Eleanor Lambert

Eleanor Lambert, who died in 2003 at the age of 100, worked long in the fashion industry to promote American designers such as Bill Blass, Oscar de la Renta, Calvin Klein, and Halston during a time when French designers were all that mattered in the fashion world. As early as the 1920s, Ms. Lambert challenged the view that Paris was the source of fashion. In 1943, to prove her point, she organized fashion shows so that the press could preview American designer collections all in one venue. These revolutionary shows were the ancestors of today's New York Fashion Week.

Source: *Chicago Sun-Times*

guages. Writing is an important part of public relations, so you should build your writing skills, perhaps by working on school publications.

In college, pursue a degree in public relations, English, journalism, or business. A graduate degree is often required for top positions. Some companies have training programs for newly hired PR specialists. In other companies, new employees work closely under the supervision of more experienced specialists. They read and file newspaper and magazine articles, perform research, and learn to write press releases.

Earnings

Public relations specialists, especially those employed by large fashion houses and companies, can earn high salaries. Earnings will vary, however, depending on an individual's experience, education, and responsibilities within the company.

Public relations specialists had median annual earnings of $41,710 in 2002. Salaries ranged from less than $24,240 to more than $75,100. Specialists with many years of experience

FOR MORE INFO

For career information and PR news, contact
Council of Public Relations Firms
100 Park Avenue, Suite 1600
New York, NY 10017
Tel: 877-773-4767
http://www.prfirms.org

For statistics, salary surveys, and other information about the profession, contact
Public Relations Society of America
33 Irving Place
New York, NY 10003
Tel: 212-995-2230
http://www.prsa.org

can earn as much as $100,000 or more. These executives may serve as a company vice president or in other managerial positions.

Outlook

Employment growth for PR professionals is expected to be much faster than the average. Competition is strong for beginning jobs, and people with both education and experience will have an advantage. For fashion PR jobs, individuals with both PR skills and previous experience in fashion retail should have an advantage.

Most large fashion employers have some sort of public relations resource, either through their own staff or through the use of an outside PR company. Even small fashion businesses will continue to need help communicating their image to the public, so PR workers should stay in demand in coming years.

Fashion Writers and Editors

What Fashion Writers and Editors Do

Fashion writers, also known as *fashion reporters, correspondents,* or *authors,* express in words their ideas about fashion. Their writing appears in books, magazines, newspapers, advertisements, radio, television, and the Internet. These writing jobs require a combination of creativity and hard work.

Fashion magazines employ the majority of fashion writers. These writers report on fashion news, conduct interviews of top designers, or write feature articles on the latest styles for a season. Fashion writers also work for newspapers with fashion sections (often a part of a larger arts-and-entertainment department), websites, or other media outlets.

Good fashion writers gather as much information as possible about their subject and then carefully check the accuracy of their sources. This can involve extensive library research, interviews, and long hours of observation and personal experience. Writers usually keep notes from which they prepare an outline or summary. They use this outline to write a first draft and then rewrite sections of their material, always searching for the best way to express their ideas. Generally, their writing

> ### Looks for 2004
>
> According to fashion writers and editors at MSNBC, these trends were hot in 2004:
> - anything in bright colors, such as red, pink, or orange
> - patterned designs—the wilder the better
> - fur—fake or real
>
> Source: MSNBC.com

will be reviewed, corrected, and revised many times before a final copy is ready for publication.

Fashion editors work with fashion writers on the staffs of newspapers, magazines, publishing houses, radio or television stations, and corporations of all kinds. Their primary responsibility is to make sure that the text that fashion writers provide is suitable in content, format, and style for the intended audiences. For example, a fashion editor working for a newspaper would ensure that articles are timely and can be understood and enjoyed by the newspaper's average reader—not just people in the fashion industry.

Editors must make sure that all text to be printed is well written, factually correct (sometimes this job is done by a *researcher* or *fact checker*), and grammatically correct. Other editors, including managing editors, editors in chief, and editorial directors, have managerial responsibilities and work with heads of other departments, such as marketing, sales, and production.

EXPLORING

○ To improve your writing skills, read, read, read. Read all kinds of writing—not just fashion articles. Fiction, nonfiction, poetry, and essays will introduce you to many different forms of writing.

○ Work as a reporter, writer, or editor on school newspapers, yearbooks, and literary magazines.

○ Start a journal and write in it every day. Express yourself freely.

Education and Training

Writers and editors usually need to have completed a college education, generally in communications, English, or journalism. They should also know how to use a computer for word processing and be able to meet deadlines. Fashion writers and editors must be knowledgeable about their subject, so classes in fashion design and marketing are also useful.

Earnings

Beginning fashion writers' salaries range from $20,000 to $26,000 per

Good Writing Takes Practice

Fashion writers and editors need to be creative and unique—which takes practice. To keep your own creative juices flowing, try these critical thinking and writing exercises.

○ Pick one of your favorite books to review. What is it about the book that you like? The plot? The author's writing style? The characters?

○ Find a fashion article in a newspaper or magazine. Describe what the article is about. Does the article include photographs? If so, what do they add to the piece? If the fashion writer states opinions about new fashion styles, do you agree or disagree? Why? Would you write the article differently? If so, how?

year. More experienced writers may earn between $28,000 and $38,000. Best-selling authors may make well over $100,000 per year, but they are few in number.

The salaries of fashion magazine editors are roughly comparable to those of book editors. A *Publishers Weekly* salary survey reported that editorial salaries in 2002 ranged from $152,750 for top editorial personnel at large publishing houses to just below $30,000 for editorial assistants at smaller companies. Beginning salaries of $20,000 or less are still common in many areas.

Outlook

Employment opportunities in writing and editing are expected to increase at a faster than average rate for the next decade. Jobs should be available at newspapers, magazines, book publishers, advertising agencies, businesses, websites, and nonprofit organizations. The best opportunities for employment should be in small newspapers, radio stations, and television stations. In these organizations, pay is low even by the standards of the publishing business.

However, because fashion writing and editing is a very specific market, competition for these jobs will be very intense. Individuals with previous experience and specialized education in fashion and reporting will be the most successful at finding jobs.

FOR MORE INFO

This organization of book publishers offers an extensive website for people interested in learning more about the book business.

Association of American Publishers
71 Fifth Avenue, Second Floor
New York, NY 10003
Tel: 212-255-0200
http://www.publishers.org

This organization is a good source of information on internships and the magazine industry.

Magazine Publishers of America
810 Seventh Avenue, 24th Floor
New York, NY 10019
http://www.magazine.org

Visit this site for information on careers in fashion writing and editing and school listings:

Fashion-Schools.org
http://www.fashion-schools.org

The Slot is a website founded and maintained by Bill Walsh, a copy editor at the Washington Post. Walsh's tips on proper word usage, grammar lessons, and style guides are not only informative, but also funny.

The Slot
http://www.theslot.com

To read about fashions, models, and agencies, check out this website hosted by fashion magazines Vogue and W.

Style.com
http://www.style.com

Knit Goods Industry Workers

What Knit Goods Industry Workers Do

Knit goods industry workers operate and repair the machines that knit various products, such as sweaters, socks, hats, sweatshirts, undergarments, lace, and other apparel. *Designers* create patterns and then choose the colors and yarn to make them. *Production managers* supervise the making of garments and keep track of costs and other important work records. *Knitters* and other workers actually produce the finished product.

Although some workers still knit fabrics by hand, most commercial knitting is done by machine. Machines make knitted fabrics in much the same way it is done by hand: by forming loops of yarn with needles and then stitching them together with other loops. Machines, however, can knit thousands of stitches per second and therefore produce many more items in a fraction of the time.

A Human Rights Issue

Clothing retailers' first consideration is making a profit. To do this, they need to keep their production costs down. Some large retailers that make their clothes overseas exploit their workers. These overseas factories are sometimes called "sweatshops" because some employ children, pay little wages, and are unsafe or unhealthy to work in. No Sweat is an organization working against sweatshops. Visit No Sweat's website (http://www.nosweatapparel.com) to read information about sweatshop abuses and order clothing produced by trade union members in the United States, Canada, and the developing world. No Sweat's casual clothes range from basic T-shirts to clothing with logos that take a stand for human rights.

Many knitters and other workers are needed to operate these high-speed machines. Knitters put spools of yarn onto each machine and fasten the yarn to the machine's needles. While the machine is in operation, knitters replace spools of yarn as needed and watch for any problems, such as yarn or needles breaking. Knitters are also usually responsible for keeping the machines in good working order. They grease the needles so that they run smoothly and keep the rest of the machine well oiled. If a major problem does occur, knitters may call in a specialist to repair the machine.

Knit goods workers are also needed in other areas of the production process. They prepare the yarn before it goes to the knitters and then clean and wash the fabric after it has gone through the machines. Many fabrics are then dyed with color or given special finishes to make them waterproof or wrinkle-resistant. All of the above operations are usually done by machine, but workers must mix the chemicals and watch the machines.

After the production process is completed, workers inspect the fabrics to make sure there are no flaws. Then they press the material and box it for shipping. Different workers usually fulfill these activities, but in small companies the same worker may do a variety of tasks.

Education and Training

Although a high school diploma is not always required for jobs in this industry, it is highly recommended. Take classes in art, computer science, family and consumer science, mathematics, and English.

The best way to become a knit goods industry worker is to complete

EXPLORING

○ Talk to your parents or a teacher about touring a knitting mill. If you do not live near one, consider contacting a knit goods industry worker who is located elsewhere and conduct an informational interview over the phone.
○ To learn about machine repair, consider joining a club that focuses on mechanics.
○ Take up knitting, needlepoint, or sewing to learn about the yarns, needles, machines, and other equipment knit goods industry workers use.

Learn More about It

Bergh, Rene. *Kids' Clothes Sew Easy: Easy to Sew T-Shirts, Track-suits, Leggings, Trousers, Shorts, Dungarees, Anoraks, Skirts, and Dresses*. London: New Holland Publishers, 2003.

Christensen, Jo Ippolito. *The Needlepoint Book: A Complete Update of the Classic Guide*. New York: Fireside/Penguin Group, 1999.

Clewer, Caroline. *Kids Can Knit: Fun and Easy Projects for Small Knitters*. Hauppauge, N.Y.: Barrons Educational Series, 2003.

Falick, Melanie. *Kids Knitting: Projects for Kids of All Ages*. New York: Black Dog & Leventhal Publishers, 1998.

Milligan, Lynda, and Nancy Smith. *Best of Sewing Machine Fun for Kids*. Concord, Calif.: C&T Publishing, 2004.

Siegler-Lathrop, Dominique. *The Secrets of Needlepoint: Technique & Stitches*. Rockport, Maine: Down East Books, 2000.

an apprenticeship program offered by textile manufacturers. These programs last from several days (for cleaners) to several months (for machine repairers). Apprenticeships include on-the-job training and courses in mathematics and machine shop practice. Many community colleges and technical schools also offer two-year programs in textile making.

Although a college degree is not necessary for most jobs in this field, those who wish to become designers or production managers usually need a college degree as well as several years of work experience. Workers can also advance through company-sponsored training programs and may go on to become instructors themselves.

Earnings

Knit goods workers' earnings vary according to the location of the mill they work in and the goods they produce. The U.S. Department of Labor reported the median hourly earnings for textile knitting and weaving machine setters, operators, and

FOR MORE INFO

For information on the manufactured fibers knit goods industry workers work with, contact

American Fiber Manufacturers Association

1530 Wilson Boulevard, Suite 690

Arlington, VA 22209

Tel: 703-875-0432

http://www.fibersource.com/afma/afma.htm

For news and general industry information, contact

American Textile Manufacturers Institute

1130 Connecticut Avenue, NW, Suite 1200

Washington, DC 20036

Tel: 202-862-0500

http://www.atmi.org

This union fights for workers' rights. It represents workers in various industries, including basic apparel and textiles.

UNITE (Union of Needle Trades, Industrial and Textile Employees)

275 Seventh Avenue

New York, NY 10001

Tel: 212-265-7000

http://www.uniteunion.org

tenders to be $11.05 in 2002. This wage translates into yearly earnings of approximately $22,980 based on a 40-hour workweek. Textile cutting machine setters, operators, and tenders earned $9.77 an hour (or $20,320 annually). Workers in hosiery plants and knit outerwear and knit underwear mills normally earn less. Many production workers in apparel manufacturing are paid according to the number of pieces they produce, so their total earnings depend on their skill, speed, and accuracy. Apprentices are normally paid wages that are somewhat lower than those of experienced employees.

Outlook

Employment prospects for knit goods workers and other textile workers are not expected to be strong. In fact, the U.S. Department of Labor predicts that there will be a decline in employment for all textile machinery operators in coming years. While the demand for knit goods has increased along with population growth, automation and overseas production have combined to keep the demand for knit goods workers low in the United States. The number of jobs in knitting mills has decreased significantly as a result of plant closings and downsizing.

Labor-saving, computerized machinery has increased productivity. Job prospects look best for skilled engineers, technicians, computer personnel, and others who know how to operate and service complex knitting machinery.

Makeup Artists

What Makeup Artists Do

Makeup artists design and apply makeup for stage and screen actors. They read scripts and meet with directors, producers, and technicians. They create special effects ranging from scars and prosthetics to radio-controlled mechanical body parts. Sometimes makeup artists apply "clean" (natural-looking) makeup and eliminate or apply wrinkles, tattoos, or scars. When they design makeup, makeup artists must consider the age of the characters, the setting and period of the film or play, and the lighting effects that will be used. Historical productions require considerable research to design hair, makeup, and fashion styles of a particular era. Makeup artists also may work on hair, but in many states locally licensed cosmetologists must be brought in for hair cutting, coloring, and perms.

Makeup artists play an important role during production. They watch the monitors constantly during filming to make sure the actors' makeup is just right. They reapply or adjust makeup as needed throughout filming or between scenes. They help the

Award-Winning Makeup Artists

In recent years, the following makeup artists took home Academy Awards for Best Makeup:

2003: Richard Taylor and Peter King for *The Lord of the Rings: The Return of the King*

2002: John Jackson and Beatrice De Alba for *Frida*

2001: Peter Owen and Richard Taylor for *The Lord of the Rings: The Fellowship of the Ring*

2000: Rick Baker and Gail Ryan for *Dr. Suess's How the Grinch Stole Christmas*

1999: Christine Blundell and Trefor Proud for *Topsy Turvy*

1998: Jenny Shircore for *Elizabeth*

(Source: Oscar.com)

A makeup artist applies makeup to a model before a fashion show. (Corbis)

actors remove makeup at the end of the day. These artists must be able to spot any makeup problems before a scene is filmed.

Most makeup artists are self-employed and work on a freelance basis. When they are not working on a film, they might work for television or video projects, commercials, and industrial films to supplement their film work. Makeup artists for the theater may be employed full time by a theater, or they may be freelancers. Makeup artists also work for photographers who do fashion photography.

Education and Training

Most makeup artists have a bachelor's or master's degree in theater, art history, photography, fashion, or a related subject. To prepare for a career as a makeup artist, take art classes, such as art history, photography, painting, drawing, and sculpting.

EXPLORING

○ Volunteer at local theaters. The summer months will offer the most opportunities. Small community theaters may allow you to explore makeup artistry.

○ Volunteer to do makeup for school productions. Take pictures of your work.

Profile: Rick Baker

In 1981, when the Academy Award for Best Makeup was introduced, Rick Baker received the first of these awards for *An American Werewolf in London*. He won his second Oscar for designing a hairy bigfoot monster in *Harry and the Hendersons* (1987) and his third Oscar for designing and creating the Bela Lugosi makeup for Martin Landau in *Ed Wood* (1994). Since then, he has garnered several more awards.

Baker was a fan of horror movies as a child. He experimented with movie makeup effects at a young age and later assisted the famous makeup artist Dick Smith. Rick Baker is considered one of the best makeup artists in the field.

Anatomy and chemistry classes will also be useful. Participate in school drama productions and assist with makeup whenever possible.

Cosmetology licenses or certificates from special makeup schools are not required, but they may help in a job search, especially when you start out. If you are willing to spend some time working for very little pay, or even for free, you can gain valuable experience assisting an experienced, established makeup artist. There are also some highly regarded schools for makeup artists, such as the Joe Blasco Schools in California and Florida.

Earnings

Makeup artists usually earn a daily rate for their services. This rate varies depending on the budget and size of the production and the experience and reputation of the makeup artist. Day rates can range from $50 for a small theater production to $1,000 for a large Broadway show or feature film. Work is rarely steady. Most makeup artists work long hours for several weeks, and then may be without work for a time.

FOR MORE INFO

To read industry news or order a copy of Make-Up Artist Magazine, *visit the following website:*

Make-Up Artist Magazine
PO Box 4316
Sunland, CA 91041
Tel: 818-504-6770
http://www.makeupmag.com

For information about theater jobs, contact

Theatre Communications Group
520 Eighth Ave, 24th Floor
New York, NY 10018
Tel: 212-609-5900
http://www.tcg.org

For information about the Joe Blasco schools and careers in makeup artistry, check out the website

Joe Blasco Makeup Training and Cosmetics
http://www.joeblasco.com

Outlook

On the whole, opportunities for makeup artists are expected to increase. Many new jobs will become available as the film and television industries continue to grow. Increased use of special effects will require makeup artists with special talent and training. The future for work in theaters is less predictable, but traveling productions and regional theaters should continue to offer plenty of employment opportunities.

Merchandise Displayers

What Merchandise Displayers Do

Merchandise displayers design and build displays for store windows, showcases, and floors. They are sometimes called *display workers, showcase trimmers,* and *window dressers*. Store displays must be artistic and attractive so that customers will want to buy the products.

Some merchandise displayers work in self-service stores, such as supermarkets. Because there are no salespeople, displays are very important in attracting the customer to buy products. In large retail stores, such as department stores, there may be a large staff of display specialists. These workers often use mannequins and other props for displaying apparel. Merchandise displayers also prepare product displays for trade shows, exhibitions, conventions, or festivals. They build installations such as booths and exhibits. They also install carpeting, drapes, and other decorations, including flags, banners, and lights, and arrange furniture and other accessories.

Displayers first develop an idea or theme that will highlight the merchandise and attract customers. Display workers use hammers, saws, spray guns, and other hand tools to build displays. They may use carpeting,

Anatomy of an Exhibit

A typical museum exhibit includes the following items:

- title
- objects (including art and artifacts)
- photographs and sketches
- object mounts, supports, and stands
- labels
- written explanations or background information
- audiovisual components
- lighting
- security features

EXPLORING

○ Help design and arrange bulletin boards, posters, or displays at school.

○ Help with decorations or publicity for school dances and parties.

○ Join your school or community drama group to work on sets, props, and costumes.

○ Help your neighbors arrange items for garage or yard sales.

○ Take art, sculpture, calligraphy, or carpentry courses offered in your community.

wallpaper, and special lighting. They build and paint the backdrops and gather all the props they'll need. Finally, they arrange merchandise and hang printed materials, such as signs, descriptions of the merchandise, and price tags.

Sometimes display workers work in teams where each worker has a specialty, such as sign making, window painting, or carpentry.

Education and Training

Merchandise displayers must have at least a high school education. Courses in art, woodworking, mechanical drawing, and merchandising are useful. Some employers expect their merchandise displayers to have college courses in art, fashion merchandising, advertising, or interior decorating.

Art institutes, fashion merchandising schools, and some junior colleges offer courses in merchandise display. Many merchandise displayers receive their training on the job. They may start as sales clerks and learn while assisting window dressers or display workers.

Earnings

According to the U.S. Department of Labor, merchandise displayers earned a median salary of $22,550 in 2002. Beginners earned $15,100 or less, and more experienced displayers earned more than $40,020 a year. Freelancers may earn as much as $50,000 a year, but their income depends on their

What Exhibit Designers Do

Exhibit designers plan and design displays in museums. They arrange artifacts and objects, or create scenes from other times and places. Along with the objects, they arrange text and other information to explain the display items to viewers.

Exhibit designers meet regularly with curators, educators, and conservators throughout the planning stages. Each exhibit must be educational, and the team plans each exhibition so that it tells a story. They use informative labels, group objects logically, and construct displays that place objects in their proper context.

Exhibit designers must also think about keeping objects safe from harm caused by light, temperature, and movement. Most permanent exhibits are planned four years in advance while temporary exhibits take between six and 18 months to prepare.

Museums usually hire exhibit designers who have at least a bachelor's degree in art or design. Courses in museum studies are also helpful.

Although design jobs are expected to grow faster than the average, the opportunities for exhibit designers may be limited. Many museums rely on grants for funding, so they often face budget problems. Exhibit designers may find more opportunities with private exhibition and design firms.

FOR MORE INFO

This organization offers information on interior design, including school listings and details on career specialties.

American Society of Interior Designers
608 Massachusetts Avenue, NE
Washington, DC 20002

Tel: 202-546-3480
http://www.asid.org

To read about industry news and see the latest design ideas, check out the following magazine's website:

Display & Design Ideas
http://www.ddimagazine.com

reputation, number of clients, and number of hours they work. Display managers in big-city stores earn more.

Outlook

The employment of display workers is expected to grow at an average rate. Retail businesses continue to grow and will need merchandisers to help sell products.

Personal Shoppers

What Personal Shoppers Do

Personal shoppers help people who do not have the time or the ability to go shopping for clothes, gifts, groceries, and other items. Personal shoppers shop at department stores, look at catalogs, and surf the Internet for the best buys and most appropriate items for their clients.

Personal shoppers might do grocery shopping and run other errands for senior citizens or people with disabilities. Shoppers may also help professionals create an appropriate, complete wardrobe. Whatever the shopping assignment, they rely on their knowledge of the local marketplace in order to shop quickly and efficiently.

Some personal shoppers specialize in a particular area. For example, someone with a background in cosmetology may work as *image consultants,* advising clients on their hair, clothes, and makeup and shopping for clothing and beauty products.

Personal shoppers who offer wardrobe consultation visit their clients' homes and evaluate their clothes. Shoppers help determine what additional clothes and accessories they need and offer advice on

Offbeat Websites

The Internet has revolutionized the way many people shop. You can browse the Web to get listings of clearance sales across the country, place bids at cyber-auctions, and skim directories of outlet malls. But here are a few unusual sources that you are less likely to use in your personal shopping career:

○ Order logs for log homes at Wholesale Log Homes, Inc. (http://www.wholesaleloghomes.com)
○ Get fresh caviar at wholesale prices at Caviar-Express. (http://www.caviarexpress.org)
○ Golf addicts with limited budgets can benefit from the savings at http://www.golfballs.com.
○ Save 50 to 70 percent on that final purchase of your life at http://www.directcasket.com.

what items to wear together. With their clients, personal shoppers come up with a budget and start shopping at stores or on the Internet.

Personal shoppers may receive very specific instructions on what to purchase, or they may have to think of gift ideas themselves after interviewing the client and discussing the recipient's tastes. Some shoppers run other errands, such as purchasing theater tickets, making deliveries, dropping off laundry, and going to the post office.

Education and Training

Take classes in home economics to develop budget and consumer skills as well as learn about fashion and home design. Math, business, and accounting courses will prepare you for the administrative details of the job. Negotiation skills may be useful.

Many people working as personal shoppers have had experience in other areas of business. They've worked as managers in corporations or as salespeople in retail clothing stores. But there isn't any specific education or training required for this career. A small-business course at a local community college, along with classes in design, fashion, and consumer science, can help you develop the skills you'll need for the job.

Earnings

Personal shoppers bill their clients in different ways: they set a regular fee for services, charge a percentage of

EXPLORING

- Go to a mall and study other people's buying habits. Do people linger longer in certain stores? Do they try on a lot of items only to walk out? Think of ways you could make the shopping experience easier for people with limited time.
- Learn about budgeting, comparison pricing, and negotiating.
- If you are old enough to apply for a part-time job, consider working at a retail store to learn more about selling merchandise and assisting customers.

Learn More about It

Before you go spending other people's money, you should have a good sense of your own. Check out these books to learn money-saving tips and become master of your own bank.

Burkett, Larry. *Money Matters for Teens Workbook: Age 11–14.* Chicago: Moody Press, 1998.

Harman, Hollis Page. *Money Sense for Kids!* Hauppauge, N.Y.: Barrons Juveniles, 1999.

Karlitz, Gail, and Debbie Honig. *Growing Money: A Complete Investing Guide for Kids.* New York: Price Stern Sloan, 1999.

Mayr, Diane. *The Everything Kids' Money Book: From Saving to Spending to Investing: Learn All About Money!* Avon, Mass.: Adams Media Corporation, 2002.

Otfinoski, Steve. *The Kid's Guide to Money: Earning It, Saving It, Spending It, Growing It, Sharing It.* New York: Scholastic, 1996.

the sale, or charge an hourly rate. Or, they might use all these methods in their business. Their billing method may depend on the client and the service. For example, when offering wardrobe consultation and shopping for clothes, a personal shopper may find it best to charge by the hour; when shopping for a small gift, it may be more reasonable to charge only a percentage. Personal shoppers charge anywhere from $25 to $125 an hour. The average hourly rate is about $75. Successful shoppers working in a large city can make between $1,500 and $3,000 a month.

Outlook

Personal shopping is fairly new, so anyone embarking on the career will be taking some serious risks. There's not a lot of research available about the career and no real sense of the career's future. The success of Internet commerce will probably have a big effect on the future of personal shopping. Some personal shoppers who have websites offer consultation via email and help people purchase products online.

FOR MORE INFO

To learn about careers as professional organizers, contact

National Association of Professional Organizers
4700 West Lake Avenue
Glenview, IL 60025
Tel: 847-375-4746
http://www.napo.net

Global Image Group helps individuals and corporations sharpen their images through consulting and personal shopping services. Visit their website to learn more about this type of personal shopping and image consulting.

Global Image Group
http://www.globalimagegrp.com

Photo Stylists

What Photo Stylists Do

Photo stylists work with photographers, art directors, models, and clients to create a visual image. They use props, backgrounds, accessories, food, linens, clothing, costumes, and other set elements to create these images. Much of the work they do is for catalogs and newspaper advertising. Stylists also work on films and television commercials.

Most stylists specialize in fashion, food, hair and makeup, or bridal styling. Some do only prop shopping or location searches. Others prefer to develop a variety of skills so they can find different kinds of photo styling work.

Photo stylists use their imagination, resourcefulness, and artistic skills to set up a shot that will help sell a product. For example, a mail-order clothing company may want a series of ads to sell their winter line of clothing. Photo stylists may decide to design a set outside with a snow background or indoors near a fireplace with holiday decorations in the background. They gather props, such as lamps or table decorations. They rent chairs and couches to decorate the set where the shoot will take place. For an outdoor scene, they might use a sled or skiing equipment. Photo stylists hire models to wear clothing. They may work with other

Tools of the Trade

Here are some of the things photo stylists might carry with them to photo shoots:

- utility knife
- cloth steamer
- skewers
- toothpicks
- brushes
- cotton swabs
- tweezers
- glycerine
- oil
- spray bottles
- eye droppers
- blow torch
- mixer
- pastry bags and tips
- safety pins
- needle and thread
- tape

photo stylists and assistants to style the hair and makeup of the models.

Photo stylists usually have a "bag of tricks" that will solve problems or create certain visual effects. This kit may include everything from duct tape to cotton wadding to a spare salt shaker. Sometimes photo stylists build and design props from scratch. They may have to coordinate the entire production from finding the location to arranging accommodations. The best photo stylists are versatile and creative enough to come up with ideas and solutions on the spot. If they cannot create or locate something, they have many contacts who can help them out.

Photo stylists must be organized. They must make sure to gather everything that they need for a photo shoot and be sure that all materials are well cared for. After the shoot, photo stylists make sure that all borrowed items are returned and that all rentals and other transactions have been recorded.

EXPLORING

○ A backyard photo shoot can be a good way to learn the elements involved with this career.

○ Watch someone prepare a display in a department store window. Many stylists start out as window dressers.

○ Work on set design or props for a school or community theater.

○ Join a photography club and learn the basics of taking pictures.

Education and Training

There is no specific training or schooling required for photo stylists, but there are other ways to prepare for this job. Art classes can help train your eye for design and composition. Experience with building and constructing displays will be of great help. (See the chapter on merchandise displayers.) Sewing skills are necessary, especially in fashion photo design, to make minor alterations to fabrics. Those interested in hair and makeup styling should take courses in cosmetology. Interior design courses will help you arrange room settings. A general

Styling Specialties

These are some of the specialties in photo styling:

- beds and domestics
- bridal
- casting
- catalogs
- children
- fashion
- film, videos, and commercials
- food
- hair and makeup
- home furnishings
- illustration
- lifestyle
- locations
- production coordination
- props
- set design
- soft goods
- still life
- tabletop
- visual merchandising/ display
- wardrobe

knowledge of photography, film, and lighting will help you communicate with photographers.

Most photo stylists enter the field as apprentices to established stylists. Apprentices usually work for two years or more before taking on clients on their own.

Earnings

Salaries at production houses can start as low as $8 an hour. Experienced fashion or food stylists can earn as much as $800 a day and more, depending on their reputation and the budget of the production. On average, stylists earn around $350 to $500 per day as freelancers. According to the Association of Stylists and Coordinators, assistant photo stylists earn about $150 to $200 a day.

Outlook

Employment of photo stylists is expected to grow at an average rate. Good photo stylists are becoming more and more important

FOR MORE INFO

For more information about the work of photo stylists, contact

Association of Stylists and Coordinators
24 Fifth Avenue
New York, NY 10011
Tel: 212-780-3483
http://www.stylistsasc.com

to photographers and advertising clients. However, the employment outlook of photo stylists depends on the health of the advertising, film, and commercial photography industries.

New digital photography and photo enhancement technology may change the role of the photo stylist in the future. There may be more educational programs for photo stylists and this may increase the competition for styling assignments.

Retail Managers

What Retail Managers Do

Retail managers not only work in clothing stores, but they also work in supermarkets, department stores, gift shops, bakeries, and any other type of shop. But because this book deals with fashion careers, the focus here will be on clothing store managers.

Managers are in charge of everything that takes place in the store, from hiring and managing employees to ensuring that displayed clothes are neatly folded and attractively arranged. They also are responsible for the money that is made in the shop. They make sure that all receipts are tallied up, cash in the register is counted, and all is put safely away at the end of each working day. The manager is often the first to arrive in the morning and the last to leave at night.

The most important skill for a good retail manager is knowing how to work with other people. Managers hire and train employees, assign their duties, and review salaries. There are bound to be disagreements and clashes from time to time, and managers must be able to keep arguments from getting out of control. Similarly, the store's customers may have complaints, and managers must be sensitive and understanding in dealing with the public.

Whether they deal in clothing, shoes, or accessories, retail managers track all the merchandise in their stores. They keep accurate records so

On the Web

Check out the website for *Stores* (http://www.stores.org), published by the National Retail Federation. The site includes industry statistics, sales trends, and other articles on the retail field.

they know when to order new items, which items are the most popular, and which items are not selling.

Some managers handle all advertising and product promotions themselves, while others meet with advertising agency representatives and decide how best to advertise their store's merchandise. Managers often have the final say about which advertisements are sent to newspapers, radio, and television.

Other duties vary depending on the size of the store and the type of merchandise sold. In small stores, managers perform such duties as data processing, shipping, accounting, and sales. In large stores, managers may be responsible for a specific area, such as customer service or personnel.

Education and Training

Although some retail managers do not have a college education, many large retail stores accept applications only from college graduates. If you are interested in this career, study English, advertising, accounting, business, and marketing. All managers, regardless of their education, must have good marketing, analytical, and people skills.

Many large retail stores and national chains offer formal training programs, including classroom instruction, for their new employees. The training period may last a week or as long as a year. Training for a department store manager, for example, may include working as a salesperson in several departments in order to learn more about the store's business.

Part-time or summer jobs are good ways to enter this field. Often retail managers are looking for salespeople because the turnover rate in these jobs

EXPLORING

○ Test out your retail sales skills by working at your local mall. If you are too young for part-time work and know someone who owns a retail business, ask if you can volunteer.

○ Volunteer to work at a sales booth at a school event such as a play, bake sale, or basketball game.

> ## More Shopping Online
>
> Though many are still shopping the old-fashioned way by visiting retail stores for all their fashion needs, more and more shoppers are purchasing everything from shoes to shirts online. During the third quarter of 2003, U.S. retail online shopping sales reached over $13 billion—27 percent higher than for the same period in 2002.
>
> Source: U.S. Census Bureau

is quite high. A salesperson who stays with a company and takes increasing responsibility is more likely to advance into a management position.

Earnings

Salaries depend on the size of the retail store, the responsibilities of the job, and the number of customers served. According to the U.S. Department of Labor, median annual earnings of supervisors of retail sales workers, including commission, were $29,700 in 2002. Salaries ranged from less than $18,380 to more than $55,810 per year. Those who managed clothing stores in particular had average annual earnings of $30,510, and department store managers earned $29,500. Managers who oversee an entire region for a retail chain can earn more than $100,000.

In addition to a salary, some stores offer their managers special bonuses, or commissions, which are typically connected to the store's performance. Many managers also receive employee discounts on store merchandise.

Outlook

Employment for retail managers is expected to grow slower than the average for all occupations through the next decade.

FOR MORE INFO

For materials on educational programs in the retail industry, contact
National Retail Federation
325 7th Street, NW, Suite 1100
Washington, DC 20004
Tel: 800-673-4692
http://www.nrf.com

For information on jobs in retail, contact
Retail Industry Leaders Association
1700 North Moore Street, Suite 2250
Arlington, VA 22209
Tel: 703-841-2300
http://www.retail-leaders.org

Competition for jobs probably will continue to increase, and computerized systems for inventory control may reduce the need for some types of managers. Applicants with the best educational backgrounds and work experience will have the best chances of finding jobs.

Retail Sales Workers

What Retail Sales Workers Do

Retail sales workers assist customers in retail stores. In the fashion world, they help customers decide what clothes, shoes, and other wearable accessories to buy, help them try on garments, ring up sales, and take payment. Some other names for retail sales workers are *sales clerks, retail clerks,* and *salespeople.*

A retail sales worker may have a wide range of duties. In a small retail store, the sales worker may take inventory, place newspaper ads, order and price apparel, fold or hang clothes, handle telephone calls, open the store in the morning, and lock it up at night. In a large department store, retail sales workers usually work in one department (such as junior fashions) and have more limited duties.

Assisting customers is the priority for most retail sales workers. They help customers find specific items or suggest alternate choices. They may help customers put outfits together, find different sizes, and recommend certain brands or looks. When they are not waiting on customers, retail workers put price tags on items, stock the store, straighten clothes shelves and racks, clean products, and make sure aisles are clear.

With good skills, retail sales workers can move up to any of several positions. Some become the *senior salesperson* or a *department head.* They manage the other employees in the department and may be responsible for placing orders for new merchan-

Check It Out

Visit this PBS website to read about the origins of fashion and browse other fun articles. http://www.pbs.org/newshour/on2/fashion.html

A sales worker rings up a scarf for a customer in a clothing store. (Corbis)

dise. With experience, retail workers can also become floor managers, branch managers, and general managers. Some sales workers move on to become *buyers*, who decide what clothing and other merchandise the store will carry and purchase these items.

Some retail sales workers have a 40-hour workweek. In many stores, however, sales workers work 44 or 48 hours a week. Evenings and weekend work is often required, as is working long hours of overtime during the holiday season in December, when stores are at their busiest. Workers in many stores have to stay past closing time to clean up the sales floor after a busy day.

Education and Training

Employers generally hire retail workers who are at least high school graduates, although there are some

EXPLORING

○ Develop your customer service skills. Volunteer to work at a hospital gift shop or work a ticket booth at your next school play.
○ Participate in fund-raising activities, such as bake sales, candy sales, and rummage sales.

A Famous Name

Some people buy clothes just for the label that is on it. What is the most popular label? Ralph Lauren. Not bad for a guy who never went to school for fashion design. He entered his line of work as a sales worker!

part-time opportunities available to high school students. Entry-level employees sometimes are asked to work in the store's stockroom at first so that they can learn more about the store's products and operations. They also may be asked to help set up displays or assist in the customer service department. After several months they may be promoted to sales workers.

Many employers prefer to hire college graduates, especially those with degrees in merchandising, business, or liberal arts. College graduates are more likely to be put directly into the store's management training program. Job applicants with previous retail sales experience also are considered good candidates for management training.

Earnings

Most beginning sales workers start at the federal minimum wage, which was $5.15 an hour when this book was written. (To check the current federal minimum wage, visit http://www.dol.gov/dol/topic/wages/minimumwage.htm.) Wages vary greatly, depending primarily on the size and type of store and the degree of skill required. Larger retail stores might be able to offer higher wages to attract and retain their best workers. Some sales workers make as much as $12 an hour or more.

Department stores or retail chains might pay more than smaller stores. Many sales workers also receive a commission (a portion of the total amount of merchandise sold—often 4 to

FOR MORE INFO

For materials on educational programs in the retail industry, contact

National Retail Federation
325 7th Street, NW, Suite 1100
Washington, DC 20004
Tel: 800-673-4692
http://www.nrf.com

8 percent) on their sales or are paid solely on commission.

According to the U.S. Department of Labor, median hourly earnings of retail salespersons, including commission, were $8.51 in 2002. Wages ranged from less than $6.18 to more than $16.96 an hour. Sales workers in department stores earned an average of $8.79 an hour; in clothing stores, they earned $8.45 an hour.

Salespeople in many retail stores receive a discount on their own purchases, ranging from 10 to 25 percent. This privilege is sometimes extended to the worker's family.

Outlook

About 4.1 million people are employed as sales workers in retail stores of all types and sizes. Employment for sales personnel should grow about as fast as the average for all occupations in the coming years. Turnover among sales workers is much higher than average, creating a continual need to replace workers.

There should continue to be good opportunities for temporary and part-time sales workers, especially during the holidays. Stores are particularly interested in people who, by returning year after year, develop good sales backgrounds and know the store's merchandise.

Tailors and Dressmakers

What Tailors and Dressmakers Do

Tailors and dressmakers cut, sew, mend, and alter clothing. Most tailors work with menswear, such as suits, jackets, and coats. Dressmakers typically work with women's clothing, such as dresses, suits, evening wear, and wedding clothes. Tailors and dressmakers may be employed in dressmaking and custom tailor shops, department stores, dry cleaners, and garment factories. Many others are self-employed, running a small shop or taking in jobs at home.

Some tailors and dressmakers specialize in custom clothing and make garments from start to finish. They help customers choose the style and fabric, using their knowledge of the various types of fabrics. They take the customer's measurements, such as height, shoulder width, and arm length. Tailors and dressmakers may use ready-made paper patterns, though many are trained to make their own. The patterns are then placed on the fabric, and the fabric pieces are carefully cut. If the pattern is a difficult one, or if there are special fitting problems,

Types of Pins

Most modern pins are made of brass, nickel-plated steel, or stainless steel. There are different kinds of pins, each designed for a specific sewing purpose.

- **Dressmaker pins** are considered all-purpose pins, though usually they are not used for fine materials such as silk. They have regular, glass, or plastic heads.
- **Silk pins** make only small puncture holes, so they are best suited for fine silk and synthetic materials.
- **Ballpoint pins** are designed to slide between fibers, so they are best suited for knits.
- **Pleating pins** are designed for light- to medium-weight woven and knit fabrics.
- **Quilting pins** are longer and heavier pins used for heavy, bulky fabrics.
- **T-pins** are used for crafts and for pinning heavy fabrics. Their heads are long and flat, giving the pin a T shape.
- **Sequin pins** are short and are primarily used for pinning sequins and beads.

the tailor or dressmaker may cut the pattern from muslin and fit it to the customer. Adjustments are made and transferred to the paper pattern before it is used to cut the actual fabric. The cut pieces are basted together first and then sewn by hand or machine. Fittings are held to make sure the garment fits the customer properly. Afterwards the garment is finished with hems, buttons, trim, and a final pressing.

Tailors and dressmakers employed at larger shops may be trained to specialize in a specific task such as patternmaking, cutting, fitting, or sewing. *Bushelers* work in factories to repair flaws and correct imperfect sewing in finished garments. *Shop tailors* have a detailed knowledge of special tailoring tasks. They use shears or a knife to trim and shape the edges of garments before sewing, attach shoulder pads, and sew lining in coats. *Skilled tailors* put fine stitching on lapels and pockets, make buttonholes, and sew on trim.

Workers in this field must have the ability to sew very well (both by hand and machine), follow directions, and measure accurately. In addition to these skills, tailors and dressmakers must have a good eye for color and style. They must know how to communicate with and satisfy customers. Strong interpersonal skills will help tailors and dressmakers get and keep clients.

Education and Training

To prepare for a career in this field, high school home economics classes such as sewing and tailoring will be helpful. There are also many schools that offer on-site or home study courses in sewing and dressmaking. Mathematics and art classes can help in measuring and drawing sketches and designs.

EXPLORING

○ Take sewing classes at school. Your local park district or fabric and craft stores often offer lessons year-round.

○ Create and sew your own designs or offer your mending and alteration services to your family and friends.

○ Visit department stores, clothing specialty stores, and tailor's shops to observe workers involved in this field.

Origins of the Sewing Machine

It took more than one individual's ingenuity to develop the greatest sewing invention of all time—the sewing machine.

○ Thomas Saint designed a machine in 1790 that could work with leather and canvas. However, he built only a patent model and never mass-produced his invention.

○ Barthelemy Thimonnier's invention, built in 1829, is considered the first practical sewing machine. Made entirely of wood, and using a barbed needle, this machine was able to sew a chain stitch. Thimonnier mass-produced his machines and was under contract with the French government to sew army uniforms. Local tailors, afraid of the competition, raided his shop and destroyed his sewing machines. Thimonnier was able to save one machine and fled to America.

○ Elias Howe is commonly credited with inventing the first practical sewing machine in 1844 and patenting it in 1846. After marketing his machine abroad, Howe returned to America and found many other companies had infringed on his patent. He successfully sued.

○ Isaac Merrit Singer did much for the industry by mass producing the sewing machine. He also allowed the public to purchase machines on credit and implemented an aggressive sales campaign. In 2001, Singer celebrated its 150-year anniversary.

Most tailors and dressmakers have at least a high school education. However, many employers prefer college graduates with advanced training in sewing, tailoring, draping, pattern-making, and design. A limited number of schools and colleges located in the United States offer this type of training. Consider enrolling in such programs, especially if you plan to expand your career from tailoring to design.

Many tailors and dressmakers receive their training from apprenticeships offered by custom tailor shops or garment manufacturers. Many others get their start from work in related jobs, such as an alterer in a custom tailoring shop or dry cleaner store.

Earnings

Salaries for tailors and dressmakers vary widely, depending on experience, skill, and location. The median annual salary for

FOR MORE INFO

For information on careers in the apparel manufacturing industry, contact
American Apparel and Footwear Association
1601 North Kent Street, Suite 1200
Arlington, VA 22209
Tel: 800-520-2262
http://www.americanapparel.org

For a listing of home-study institutions offering dressmaking courses, contact
Distance Education and Training Council
1601 18th Street, NW
Washington, DC 20009
Tel: 202-234-5100
http://www.detc.org

For information packets on college classes in garment design and sewing, contact the following schools:
Fashion Institute of Design and Merchandising
919 South Grand Avenue
Los Angeles, CA 90015
Tel: 800-624-1200
http://www.fidm.com

Fashion Institute of Technology
Seventh Avenue at 27th Street
New York, NY 10001
Tel: 212-217-7999
http://www.fitnyc.suny.edu

tailors, dressmakers, and custom sewers is $10.68, or $22,220 a year for full-time work. Earnings ranged from a low of $6.97 an hour ($14,500 a year) to a high of $17.93 an hour ($37,290 a year).

Workers employed by large companies and retail stores receive benefits such as paid holidays and vacations, health insurance, and pension plans. They are often affiliated with one of the two labor unions of the industry—the International Ladies Garment Workers Union and the Amalgamated Clothing and Textile Workers of America—which may offer additional benefits. Self-employed tailors and dressmakers and small-shop workers usually provide their own benefits.

Outlook

Employment prospects in this industry are expected to decline in coming years. The low cost and ready availability of factory-made clothing and the invention of computerized sewing and cutting machines will contribute to this decline. Also, the apparel industry has declined in this country as many businesses choose to produce their items abroad. Tailors and dressmakers who do reliable and skillful work, however, particularly in the areas of mending and alterations, should be able to find employment.

Textile Manufacturing Workers

What Textile Manufacturing Workers Do

Textiles are woven fabrics. They are used to make anything from the clothes we wear to the rugs on our floors. *Textile manufacturing workers* are the people involved with converting natural and manufactured fibers into usable products. Some workers operate machinery that makes the fiber and yarn used to produce fabrics. Others are employed in the areas of design, research, and marketing. Textile workers' specific responsibilities depend on the area in which they work.

The textile manufacturing process begins with the preparation of fibers for spinning. *Operators* oversee machines that break up large quantities of fibers, remove some of the damaged fibers, and blend the rest of the fibers together into spools of yarn. This yarn is then fastened onto other machines, where textile workers weave it into large sheets. While the machines are in operation, operators replace spools of yarn as needed and watch for any problems, such as breaking yarn or dull needles.

The woven material may be either plain or patterned. Some textile workers set up the looms, and others make sure the pattern is developing correctly.

In other areas of the production process, workers clean and wash the

Check It Out

Visit UNITE's Kid Page (http://www.uniteunion.org/kids/kids.html) for stories and ways to get politically involved against the use of inhumane sweatshops to mass-produce clothing.

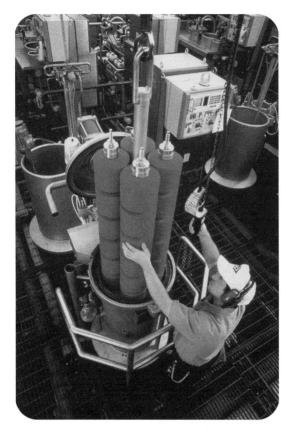

A textile manufacturing worker adjusts yard dyeing vats in a textile factory. (Corbis)

fabric after it has gone through the spinning machines, and many fabrics are dyed with color or given special finishes that make them waterproof or wrinkle resistant.

Inspectors examine the fabrics to make sure there are no flaws. Other workers iron the material and box the finished product for shipment.

A number of other workers are employed in the textile industry. *Designers* create patterns and then choose the colors and yarn to make those patterns. *Production managers* supervise the making of the garments and keep track of costs and other important work records. *Machine repair workers* fix any major problems and do maintenance tasks such as greasing and oiling the machines.

Education and Training

If you are interested in a textile career, in high school you should take courses in physics, chemistry, mathematics, and English. Computer science, shop, and family and consumer science classes will also be helpful.

A high school diploma plus some technical training is expected of job applicants in this industry. A two-year associate's degree in textile technology is required for technicians, laboratory testers, and supervisory personnel. Some companies even require a four-year degree. Most textile workers undergo a period of on-the-job training by experienced workers or representatives of equipment manufacturers. During this time, they learn the procedures and systems of their particular company.

Earnings

Earnings of textile industry workers vary depending on the type of plant where they are employed and the workers' job responsibilities, the shift they work, and seniority. The following are median salaries for workers in the industry: full-time textile bleaching and dyeing machine operators, $20,800; textile cutting machine operators, $20,320; textile knitting and weaving machine operators, $22,970; and textile winding, twisting, and drawing-out machine operators, $21,920.

EXPLORING

○ Tour a textile plant. If possible, arrange to talk to a few workers there about their jobs and how they got into the textile industry.
○ Join a sewing club, either at school or in your community.

In general, salaries generally increase with more education and greater responsibility. Some companies offer their employees discounts on the textiles or textile products they sell.

Outlook

It is predicted that there will be a decline in employment in this field in the next decade, even as the demand for textile prod-

Did You Know?

○ Recycled soda bottles and plastic food containers are being used to make fabric, such as denim.
○ The Jarvik-7 artificial heart is made up of more than 50 percent textile fiber.
○ The artificial kidney used in dialysis is made up of about 5,000 to 10,000 hollow fibers, yet it is only about two inches in diameter.
○ More than 75 percent of a tire's strength comes from textiles.

Source: American Textile Manufacturers Institute

FOR MORE INFO

Contact the ATMI for descriptive materials and audiovisual presentations on the textile industry.

American Textile Manufacturers Institute (ATMI)
1130 Connecticut Avenue, NW, Suite 1200
Washington, DC 20036
Tel: 202-862-0500
http://www.atmi.org

For information on degree and continuing education programs in textile technology, contact

North Carolina Center for Applied Textile Technology
PO Box 1044
7220 Wilkinson Boulevard
Belmont, NC 28012
Tel: 704-825-3737
http://www.nccatt.org

This union fights for workers' rights and represents workers in various industries, including basic apparel and textiles.

UNITE (Union of Needle Trades, Industrial and Textile Employees)
275 Seventh Avenue
New York, NY 10019
Tel: 212-265-7000
http://www.uniteunion.org

ucts increases. Changes in the textile industry will account for much of this decline. Factories are changing production operations and installing machines that rely more on computers than people to run them. New technology enables one person to operate several machines, whereas before several workers might be needed for one machine. Also, in the coming years there will be an increase in imports of textiles from other countries. Workers who have good technical training and skills will have the best job opportunities.

Glossary

accredited   approved as meeting established standards for providing good training and education; usually given by an independent organization of professionals to a school or a program in a school

apprentice   person who is learning a trade by working under the supervision of a skilled worker; apprentices often receive classroom instruction in addition to their supervised practical experience

associate's degree   academic rank or title granted by a community or junior college or similar institution to graduates of a two-year program of education beyond high school

bachelor's degree   academic rank or title given to a person who has completed a four-year program of study at a college or university; also called an undergraduate degree or baccalaureate

career   occupation for which a worker receives training and has an opportunity for advancement

certified   approved as meeting established requirements for skill, knowledge, and experience in a particular field; people are certified by the organization of professionals in their field

college   higher education institution that is above the high school level

community college   public two-year college, attended by students who do not usually live at the college; graduates of a community college receive an associate's degree and may transfer to a four-year college or university to complete a bachelor's degree

diploma certificate or document given by a school to show that a person has completed a course or has graduated from the school

distance education type of educational program that allows students to take classes and complete their education by mail or the Internet

doctorate academic rank or title (the highest) granted by a graduate school to a person who has completed a two- to three-year program after having received a master's degree; also known as doctor of philosophy degree, or Ph.D.

financial aid scholarships, loans, and grants provided by government agencies, academic institutions, and professional associations and organizations for academic study

fringe benefit payment or benefit to an employee in addition to regular wages or salary; examples of fringe benefits include a pension, a paid vacation, and health or life insurance

graduate school school that people may attend after they have received their bachelor's degree; people who complete an educational program at a graduate school earn a master's degree or a doctorate

grant financial aid for academic study that does not require repayment; usually awarded based on need

intern advanced student (usually one with at least some college training) in a professional field who is employed in a job that is intended to provide supervised practical experience for the student

junior college two-year college that offers courses like those in the first half of a four-year college program; graduates of a junior college usually receive an associate's degree and may transfer to a four-year college or university to complete a bachelor's degree

liberal arts subjects covered by college courses that develop broad general knowledge rather than specific occupational skills; the liberal arts are often considered to include philosophy, literature and the arts, history, language, and some courses in the social sciences and natural sciences

licensed   having formal permission from the proper authority to carry out an activity that would be illegal without that permission; for example, a person may be licensed to practice medicine or to drive a car

loan   advance of funds for academic study that must be paid back—usually with interest

major (in college)   academic field in which a student specializes and receives a degree

master's degree   academic rank or title granted by a graduate school to a person who has completed a one- or two-year program after having received a bachelor's degree

online education   academic study that is performed by using a computer and the Internet

pension   amount of money paid regularly by an employer to a former employee after he or she retires from working

private   1. not owned or controlled by the government (such as private industry or a private employment agency); 2. intended only for a particular person or group; not open to all (such as a private road or a private club)

public   1. provided or operated by the government (such as a public library); 2. open and available to everyone (such as a public meeting)

regulatory   having to do with the rules and laws for carrying out an activity; a regulatory agency, for example, is a government organization that sets up required procedures for how certain things should be done

scholarship   gift of money to a student to help the student pay for further education

social studies   courses of study (such as civics, geography, and history) that deal with how human societies work

starting salary   salary paid to a newly hired employee; the starting salary is usually a smaller amount than is paid to a more experienced worker

technical college   private or public college offering two- or four-year programs in technical subjects; technical colleges offer courses in both general and technical subjects and award associate's degrees and bachelor's degrees

technician   worker with specialized practical training in a mechanical or scientific subject who works under the supervision of scientists, engineers, or other professionals; technicians typically receive two years of college-level education after high school

technologist   worker in a mechanical or scientific field with more training than a technician; technologists typically must have between two and four years of college-level education after high school

undergraduate   student at a college or university who has not yet received a degree

undergraduate degree   see **bachelor's degree**

union   organization whose members are workers in a particular industry or company; the union works to gain better wages, benefits, and working conditions for its members; also called a labor union or trade union

vocational school   public or private school that offers training in one or more skills or trades; compare **technical college**

wage   money that is paid in return for work done, especially money paid on the basis of the number of hours or days worked

Index of Job Titles

Browse and Learn More

Books

Dickerson, Kitty G., and Jeannette Jarnow. *Inside the Fashion Business*. 7th ed. Upper Saddle River, N.J.: Prentice Hall, 2002.

Frings, Gini Stephens. *Fashion: From Concept to Consumer*. 7th ed. Upper Saddle River, N.J.: Prentice Hall, 2001.

Mauro, Lucia, Kathy Siebel, and Maureen Costello. *Careers for Fashion Plates & Other Trendsetters*. 2nd ed. New York: McGraw-Hill/Contemporary Books, 2002.

Phaidon, eds. *The Fashion Book*. Boston: Phaidon Press, 1998.

Vogt, Peter, and Angelica Wojak. *Career Opportunities in the Fashion Industry*. New York: Checkmark Books, 2002.

Watson, Linda. *Vogue: Twentieth Century Fashion*. London: Carlton Books, 2002.

Websites

Elle
http://www.elle.com

Fashion Club
http://www.fashionclub.com

FashionOffice
http://www.fashionoffice.org

Fashion Planet
http://www.fashion-planet.com

Style.com
http://www.style.com